THE ETHICAL INVESTOR

THE ETHICAL INVESTOR

UNIVERSITIES AND CORPORATE RESPONSIBILITY

by
John G. Simon
Charles W. Powers
Jon P. Gunnemann

New Haven and London, Yale University Press, 1972

*Designed by Sally Sullivan
and set in IBM Selectric Press Roman type.
Printed in the United States of America by
The Carl Purington Rollins Printing-Office
of the Yale University Press.*

*Distributed in Great Britain, Europe, and Africa by
Yale University Press, Ltd., London; in Canada by
McGill-Queen's University Press, Montreal; in Latin
America by Kaiman & Polon, Inc., New York City;
in India by UBS Publishers' Distributors Pvt., Ltd.,
Delhi; in Japan by John Weatherhill, Inc., Tokyo.*

Contents

Preface

This study has its origins in a series of meetings held at Yale in 1968 and 1969 among members of the university's administration, members of the Yale Corporation (the governing body of the university), and a group of faculty and students convened by two of the authors (Messrs. Powers and Gunnemann) and Associate Chaplain Samuel N. Slie. The conferences focused on the issues raised in an article by Powers and Gunnemann, entitled "Institutions, Investments and Integrity" (*The Christian Century*, January 1969), which called on universities and other nonprofit institutions to consider the social consequences of corporate activities from which these institutions derive an endowment return. The agenda for the meetings also included a number of questions posed in subsequent memoranda prepared by Yale President Kingman Brewster and Treasurer John E. Ecklund.

At one of these sessions, in the spring of 1969, President Brewster asked a group of faculty members to consider the possibility of offering a regular academic seminar that would explore the thicket of issues—and draw upon the several academic disciplines—pertinent to investment responsibility. With the help of Professor James M. Gustafson, a plan for such a seminar was drawn up. The seminar was offered in the 1969-70 academic year, chaired by the authors, with the generous and valuable collaboration of Professors James Tobin and William C. Brainard of the economics department. The students participating in the seminar came from Yale College (seniors majoring in economics), from the Graduate School (biology, religious studies, and political science departments), and from the Law School, Divinity School, and School of Forestry. They formed themselves into teams to look into legal, economic, and administrative problems raised by the notion of socially responsible investing, and to focus on selected case-study areas (corporate involvement in South Africa, corporate impact on environmental pollution, and economic and housing needs in the Greater New Haven area).

Many issues that engaged the seminar, briefly or at length, are not addressed in the body of this report. For example, we have not dealt in depth with all aspects of the social responsibility of business corporations; nor have we attempted to resolve public policy questions arising in various subject-matter areas (South Africa, environmental protection, inflation, etc.). Even with respect to university policies, these pages are restricted in scope. We focus here on action by a university relating to the policies and practices of corporations in which the university is a stockholder. Except in passing, we have not dealt with other aspects of the social responsibility of a university—for example, in its roles as purchaser, employer, government contractor, landlord, producer of solid or gaseous wastes, and donee of wealth acquired in varying legal and moral circumstances. (We hope, however, that our discussion of investment questions will assist consideration of these other issues.)

Nor do we consider in these pages the appropriate role of the university in providing venture capital for housing, business development, or other socially beneficial projects in the area it inhabits—an issue to which the seminar generally, and one student team in particular, gave considerable attention. This question involves a group of factors different from those relating to the responsible management of corporate securities, and it deals with a set of institutional relationships different from those existing between a university and a corporation.

We therefore caution against facile application of the conclusions reached in this report to the subject of the university's hometown responsibilities. For example, while we believe that the occasions on which the university should *initiate* action or expend resources to generate corporate reform are quite limited, we doubt that its freedom of action is so circumscribed when it seeks to contribute to the improvement of conditions in its own community. We have not, however, elaborated on this point; the task of formulating policy guidelines appropriate to the university-community investment problem must be the subject of another study.

The authors wish to express their appreciation to all faculty and student participants in the seminar. In fairness to them, we note that this report is not a collective or corporate endeavor of the seminar but rather the work product of the three authors. Although we were informed, inspired, and influenced by the other members of the seminar, the responsibility for the views set forth is ours alone.

In preparing for and conducting the seminar, we received the full cooperation of the Yale administration and the Finance Committee of the Yale Corporation; indeed, the president led one of our most stimulating seminar sessions.

We are also grateful to the Ford Foundation for a grant to the university that paid for the extensive stenographic and reproduction costs associated with the seminar, for travel expenses of seminar members, and for administrative tasks involved in coordinating a seminar embracing six different schools and departments of the university and the assembly of a wide variety of teaching materials.

We received helpful criticisms of our drafts from several members of our seminar and related seminars: Jeffrey A. Burt, Richard Cass, Pamela Cook, Robert Cook, Michael Egger, Peter O. Safir, and Allen J. Zerkin; from several Yale faculty colleagues: John M. Blum, Ralph S. Brown, Jan G. Deutsch, and Charles E. Lindblom; from faculty members at other universities: Louis Loss of Harvard Law School and Donald E. Schwartz of Georgetown Law Center; from a number of college and university administrators: Edward J. Bloustein, president of Rutgers, Mary I. Bunting, president of Radcliffe, James T. Burtchaell, provost of Notre Dame, Hugh Calkins, Fellow of the Harvard Corporation, John R. Coleman, president of Haverford, James P. Dixon, Jr., president of Antioch, Harris L. Wofford, Jr., president of Bryn Mawr; and from Bevis Longstreth, Esq., of the New York Bar and H. David Rosenbloom, Esq., of the Washington, D.C., Bar. The usual exculpatory dispensations are bestowed on all these counselors, particularly since a number of them disagree with one or more of our recommendations—in the case of one reader, violently so.

Finally, we express our appreciation to Hiram Gordon and Robert Stein for legal research assistance and to Susan G. Cohen for undertaking, with great skill and devotion, the major part of the cheerless burden of getting our various drafts typed and reproduced.

1. Introduction

It was surely inevitable that the campaigns for peace, for racial and social justice, for environmental defense and consumer protection should at last assault the classic citadel of political neutrality: the American university. At a time when all institutions are being asked to undergo change in the interest of these causes, the university is not to be spared. It has been urged to do many things—from casting out ROTC to recycling its bottles—but this book focuses on what the university has been asked to do about its investments.

Schools of higher learning recently have been urged to manage their endowments so as to respond, in some fashion, to the fact that they own stock in companies which pollute or strip-mine, operate in South Africa, fail to hire or house blacks, make DDT, napalm, and unsafe cars—or take other action believed to impair the human condition. The universities may also expect to receive requests from other, rather different, constituents who wish the institution to do something about its shares in companies that trade with Eastern Europe, contribute to "radical" or "integrationist" charities, or manufacture the Pill.

From whatever direction they come, these requests seek a measure of "social responsibility" in university investments. In recent years, demands of this kind have caused considerable debate, if not turmoil, at Princeton, Cornell, Union Theological Seminary, and Wesleyan (over South Africa), at Mount Holyoke and the University of Pennsylvania (over *Campaign GM*), at Dartmouth and Union College (over Eastman Kodak minority hiring), and at Harvard (over a similar problem at Middle South Utilities).

During the 1970-71 academic year, the traffic in student demands appeared to slacken, along with other manifestations of reduced student activity in public affairs. Yet, at the same time, trustees and faculty members at a number of universities initiated or continued investigations of the investment responsibility question,[1] either anticipating a resurgence of student clamor or be-

1

lieving that the issue would be forced upon the universities even if the students kept out of it. There are substantial grounds for such a belief. In the public media and within corporate and institutional headquarters, the corporate responsibility discussion has taken on an intensity it has never had before; it has resulted in not only a profusion of announcements by business leaders, but also the initiation of studies by corporations and many institutional investors.[2] Moreover, there is little reason to doubt that special-interest or public-interest groups—conservationists, civil rights proponents, peace organizations, public-interest law firms, etc.—will continue their efforts to intrude social concerns into stockholders' meetings and corporate board rooms in the years to come. As long as the responsibility theme continues to be heard from sources inside and outside the corporation, universities that hold corporate shares will be called upon—by sources inside and outside the university—to consider what part they, as holders of $8 billion worth of corporate stock, will play in the unfolding controversy.[3]

It is not easy to generalize about the way in which universities, to date, have responded to these demands. For one thing, the data are highly fragmentary, composed of random reports of university decisions that find their way into press reports or corporate responsibility conferences. And the available information does not fit into a clear pattern.

For example, there has been a wide variety of answers to the demands for divestment of stocks in companies doing business in South Africa: some universities refused to sell any of these stocks; some have entered into divestment programs; others have done some quiet selling to get rid of the most controversial stocks; and at least one institution (Princeton) declined to adopt a general divestment policy but announced that it will not hold the securities of banks which extend credit directly to the South African government or of "companies which do a *primary* amount of their economic activity in South Africa."

Similarly, universities holding General Motors stock responded in several different ways to the shareholder proposals offered by *Campaign GM* in 1970 and 1971. This was a shareholder campaign sponsored by a nonprofit group called the Project on Corporate Responsibility, which presented proposals calling for creation of a shareholder committee on public policy (1970), expansion of the board to permit election of directors experienced in ecological, minority, and consumer issues (1970), inclusion of shareholder nominations of directors in the management's proxy materials (1971), nomination of directors by employees, dealers, and consumers (1971), and mandatory disclosure of information on minority hiring, pollution control, and safety measures (1971). Nineteen universities and colleges are known to have voted, in one or both years, for one or more of these proposals.[4] (Some of these institutions issued public statements explaining their action—in one case (Antioch) sending a delegation to the GM meeting; other schools simply voted.) Six universities, including one of those mentioned above, abstained on one or more proposals, either in 1970 or 1971.[5] Most of the foregoing institutions voted *No* on at least one of the *Campaign GM* proposals, and there were ten universities that voted against all the *Campaign GM* proposals in 1970 or 1971 or in both years.[6]

Just as the actions taken by universities have varied widely, so has the rhetoric about the investment responsibility of universities. The positions taken by various groups at Cornell in 1968 illustrate the breadth of the spectrum. A petition signed by 1,200 students declared that "Cornell University should not profit from the human degradation and misery brought about by the criminal *apartheid* system of South Africa" and therefore demanded the immediate sale of all investments in banks which have loaned money to the Republic of South Africa. Shortly thereafter, the faculty passed this resolution:

It is the sense of this Faculty, in keeping with the liberal and humane traditions of the University, that Cornell's investment policies should reflect a serious concern with the possible moral implications of those policies.

In particular, we regard the repressive and discriminatory racial policies of the government of South Africa as flagrantly in violation of the ideals of the University itself.

We therefore believe it would be both fitting and desirable for the Board of Trustees, in exercising its financial responsibilities, to try, insofar as possible, to avoid investments that significantly support, or might reasonably be construed as supporting, any such policies.

In response, the board of trustees stated that these requests "raise significant matters of University policy that will continue to command the attention of the Board of Trustees" and that "the Trustees will remain alert to these considerations . . . in the light of the fiscal and legal responsibilities of the Board of Trustees." The board rejected the petition, however, for a number of reasons also heard in other quarters:

[The reasons] . . . center on the fact that . . . Cornell University's investment in any individual company involves an insignificant fraction of that company's total financial assets; on the need for flexible management of an endowment fund . . . ; on the extreme difficulty of securing adequate information that would permit judgment about the policies of companies in which Cornell funds are invested; and on the legal responsibilities of the Trustees as fiduciaries.

A somewhat different explanation was advanced by a majority of the trustees of the Yale Corporation in 1970 when Yale abstained from voting its shares in the *Campaign GM* controversy. These trustees announced that they had acted

on the principle that the Fellows of the Corporation do not, and should not, have the power to take a corporate position on issues of a political or social nature which do not directly affect the University in its relations with the local community. . . . This principle derives from the philosophy that a university by its very nature is a collegium or forum for the expression of a wide diversity of views. This conception is the cornerstone of academic freedom.

These statements provide a sampler of the various and conflicting commandments one encounters in discussions of the university's investment responsibilities:

Do not profit from immorality.

Do not support corporate immorality.

Do not abandon fiscal and legal responsibilities.

Do not bother, for the ownership interest is too tiny.

Do not bother, for the information is too hard to get.

Do not jeopardize academic freedom by taking political or social positions.

In analyzing these and other positions bearing on a university's
investment policies, we have found that the inquiry has a pro-
found tendency to unravel. Early in our work, we discovered that
we could not weigh the demands for moral responsibility on the
part of universities without examining some first principles relating to the functions of universities and their trustees. We also
came to realize that we could not resolve the issue of the university's role without exploring various aspects of the responsibilities
of other institutions and individuals. First, we found that we
could not reach conclusions about what a university ought to do
without first exploring the question of what role *investors as a
whole* ought to play in shaping corporate behavior. (Indeed, it
was largely on this issue that the Harvard Corporation based its
decision to vote for the GM management in the 1970 GM proxy
controversy: "In our view, the Board of Directors and not the
stockholders of a corporation constitute the proper body for the
determination of difficult questions of allocation of resources.")
We then realized that the controversy over the investor's role
could not be resolved without at least some examination of the
issue of how the *corporation* as a business entity ought to respond to the calls for corporate responsibility. And when dealing
with this topic, we concluded that we could not discuss the responsibility of corporations—or, for that matter, the responsibility of investors or universities-as-investors—without attempting to
set forth some major premises about the responsibilities which all
of us should be willing to accept *as individuals* in our daily lives.

We do not purport to treat definitively or exhaustively all these
underlying questions—the mission of the university, or the social
responsibilities of investors, or of corporations, or of all persons.
We have developed each of these topics only far enough to arrive

at working conclusions that form a basis for the rest of the analysis. Even so, however, our attempt to deal with the unraveling syndrome has transformed what was to be a short monograph report into a much lengthier report—long enough at least to justify the following road map.

The ensuing chapters of this study take up these questions in a sequence which is the reverse of the order in which they are mentioned above—i.e., the reverse of the order in which they opened up for us. Thus, chapter 2 begins with a discussion of "A General View of Responsibility." Here we expound, as a point of departure, what we take to be the minimal moral responsibility that all members of society have always been asked to observe: as individuals, we recognize varying degrees of commitment to take affirmative action for social improvement, but we share the obligation not to inflict harm upon others. While, as we shall see, this injunction to prevent and correct what we call social injury is easier to state in the abstract than to translate into workaday rules, that difficulty does not obviate an honest effort to respect the prohibition. Such an effort, we believe, is required not only of individual men and women but also of the large collective institutions through which men and women function in a complex society.

Accordingly, the remainder of chapter 2 and all of chapter 3 attempt to test the application of this fundamental "negative injunction"—first, to the business activities of the *corporate entity* itself; second, to the activities of *shareholders* as investors in the corporate enterprise and third, to the activities of a *university* in its capacity as an investor.

In the course of the discussion in chapters 2 and 3, we shall encounter various notions about the conduct of corporate and university life that may seem, at first glance, to conflict with the suggestion that a corporation, or a shareholder, or a university, should consider principles of social responsibility when carrying on essentially economic activities.

At the corporate level, the proposition that business judgments must account for social consequences encounters, for example, the premise that profitability is the key to maximization and efficient allocation of national resources, and also the premise that corporate regulation is a governmental function which companies cannot undertake without being oppressive or incompetent or competitively self-destructive.

At the shareholder level, the proposal that investors should press for greater corporate responsibility encounters the premise that shareholders are not equipped to participate in a company's business decisions, the premise that the interest of any institutional or individual investor is too small to create responsibility for corporate behavior, and the somewhat contrary premise that institutional investors hold large amounts of economic power which it is dangerous to deploy.

At the university level, the proposal that the trustees should exercise shareholder rights to press for increased corporate responsibility encounters the premises that the university's essential function is to promote a climate for teaching and scholarship, that this climate must be protected against politicization or external reprisal, and that in fact universities are not well organized to make collective decisions about social or political questions.

At the university level one also encounters a separate set of premises based on law: the rules governing charitable fiduciaries—who are required to observe the "prudent man" investment rule and prohibited from violating charter provisions or gift conditions—and the tax code rules regulating exempt organizations. (These legal questions are examined in chapter 5.)

Although some of these premises are open to question, most of them represent widely accepted operating principles for the conduct of corporate and university life. And yet we conclude—in chapters 2 and 3, and (with respect to legal matters) in chapter 5—that none of these premises is powerful enough to sweep all before it; that, within corporations and universities alike, the pursuit of these principles can coexist with a deliberate and orderly consideration of the social effects of corporate or university economic activity; that what Kingman Brewster has called "the terrible tension at the moment between the imperative of university neutrality and the imperative of university morality" can be reconciled without impairing the values protected by either of these expressions. And while we note that the consideration of social consequences may improve the return from economic activity, we conclude that, even where this is not the case, the time has passed when corporations, and universities investing in corporations, can properly or even prudently ignore the impacts of income-generating activity upon the general welfare.

We believe that in all three categories (corporation, shareholder, and university) the conflict we are discussing—the conflict between the demand for responsibility and certain premises of corporate or university life—is greatly diminished where the socially responsible action represents *self-regulation* of the socially injurious consequences of income-generating activity. We have not concluded that the tension may be resolved *only* in the context of self-regulation; our analysis did not lead us to a conclusion either way on that point. But we did find it easier to deal with the conflict where the corporation, or the investor, or the university, was being asked to do no more (and no less) than obey the negative injunction to which, we believe, all men and women are bound.

The analysis that follows in chapters 2 and 3 develops in detail the reasons for this conclusion. We pause here briefly to illustrate the distinction, in these different categories, between self-regulatory and more aggressive conduct—a distinction which underlies our conclusion that self-regulation can, and should, take place even where no moral causes are affirmatively promoted. Some individuals devote themselves, on a fulltime or parttime basis, to personal or organizational campaigns to protect the environment. Others may regulate their own impacts on the ecosystem—for example, by refraining from littering the street; these individuals do not thereby "champion" the environmental cause. And neither does a corporation which reduces its own litter—although it might also engage in an affirmative campaign by purchasing television time for environmental messages. Similarly, a shareholder who tries to stop his company from littering is engaged in self-regulation rather than social crusading—unless he purchased his shares for that purpose.

In this connection, with respect to the university, compare two hypothetical institutions. The first—against its investment judgment—buys stock in the above-mentioned corporate polluter, for the purpose of forcing the company to reform itself. The second university, for economic reasons, has purchased stock in the same company and decides, for the same reasons, to retain the stock; it concludes, however, that it cannot acquiesce in the company's environmental practices by voting for the management in the face of a shareholder proxy campaign. In the first case, the university jeopardizes its economic return in order to achieve a social result, an activity for which the university is not primarily organized. Its aggressively "political" stand presents a potential conflict with the duty to maintain a tranquil academic climate and with conventional assumptions about the limited range of academic competence; there may also be a clash with the trustees' legal duty to be prudent investors. But in the second case, where the university purchases and holds the stock in order to maximize its return for educational purposes, need it approve every company practice, regardless of social consequences? Such a course of conduct, as we shall point out in chapters 3 and 5, is not compelled by law or by the major premises of university life.

This same distinction informs the investment Guidelines we have proposed in chapter 3, which are set forth in the Appendix and illustrated in the hypothetical cases set forth in chapter 4. Because it is not our purpose to urge the university to champion social or moral causes, the Guidelines do not call for investment decisions that serve as the instrumentality for an affirmative campaign to promote social goals. Thus, the Guidelines preclude the purchase of securities for the sole purpose of challenging corporate practices; they call for portfolio purchases based solely on maximum-return principles.

On the other hand, the Guidelines do require a serious effort at self-regulation. With respect to securities the university has acquired under maximum-return criteria, the Guidelines require the university to take shareholder action to deal with company practices which appear to inflict significant social injury.* *Social*

---

*As we indicate later (p. 96), the Guidelines permit—but do not require—the university to vote on shareholder proposals dealing with social *injury* is defined in the Guidelines as particularly including a violation or frustration of domestic or international legal norms meant to protect against deprivations of health, safety, or basic freedoms. The Guidelines also provide that if the proposed university action involves more than the voting of proxies or communicating with corporate management (e.g., if it involves litigation or the commencement of a proxy campaign), the university should not take such action unless the social injury appears to be "grave."

If correction of social injury (or the process of correction) reduces the return sufficiently to make the stock unattractive under conventional maximum-return criteria, the Guidelines require the university to sell the stock; securities are to be retained only for maximum-return purposes. However, in order to minimize the incidence of such a "hit-and-run" chronology, the Guidelines require that the university sell the security—instead of taking shareholder action—whenever such a chronology is likely to occur within the near future.* For the same reason, the Guidelines require sale in lieu of shareholder action whenever it appears that, in the normal course of portfolio management, the stock would be sold before any action initiated by the university could be completed. A security is not, however, to be sold because of the

---

issues *other* than the regulation of social injury,—i.e., issues relating to the internal structure of the corporation (such as shareholder democracy questions) or to affirmative social welfare programs (such as corporate charitable contributions). This option is limited, however, to voting on proposals made by other shareholders; it does not permit the university to initiate action with respect to such issues. Moreover, this option does not permit the university to vote on any proposal "which advances a position on a social or political question unrelated to the conduct of the company's business or the disposition of its assets" (such as a generalized attack on police brutality or socialized medicine). It is important to note that some issues that might initially appear not to involve social injury (particularly those that relate to the alteration of corporate structures or internal procedures) do in fact raise social injury issues. A prominent example is a shareholder resolution proposing changes in a corporation's procedures for disclosing information to the shareholders, where the information pertains to impacts on the environment or on minority groups, or to other social injury concerns.

*These two provisions, which appear to be controversial among some of our early readers, are discussed in detail at pp. 93-95.

company's socially injurious practices unless these practices are grave and unless all methods of correcting the practices have failed or appear doomed to failure.

We have not recommended a more expansive use of such divestment; in other words, we have not proposed that divestment be employed as a first-line method for correcting corporate policies, for we think it improbable that it can have that effect, as explained in chapter 2. And if divestment is not an effective technique, we see no other reason to recommend it. We have concluded that institutional decontamination—the quest for a clean portfolio—is not a supportable or even feasible goal and that the institution which sells (or eschews) a security for that reason succeeds only in turning its back on controversy and possibly impairing its economic strength.

Who will make all these decisions for the university? Our procedural recommendations (section C of the proposed Guidelines) emanate from the principle that the university will take investment action on social responsibility grounds only in response to specific social issues arising directly from the university's quest for investment revenue. Because the trustees of the university are the group that directs this revenue-producing mission, it is logical that the trustees—rather than the faculty or the administration or the students—should assume the complementary task of deciding how to police the social impact of that mission. Charging the trustees with this role should minimize any unfavorable fiscal consequences of the Guidelines policies: the trustees can more easily discharge their investment return duties if they also police the social impact, for they will be able to monitor the effect of social injury decisions on portfolio performance. Moreover, as we explain in chapter 3, assigning these decisions to the trustees reduces the tension between social responsibility action and the premises of university life.

We have sought, however, to enhance the competence of the trustees—and reduce the burden of trustee decision-making in this area—by recommending the creation of an advisory University Investments Council, comprising members drawn from the various components of the university community and including persons with skills relevant to the task of investigating and analyzing allegations of corporate irresponsibility. Where budgetary considerations permit, the council would be assisted by a paid full-time or parttime research director. The council would entertain all questions or complaints concerning the social implications of the university's holdings, collect and analyze pertinent data as well as the viewpoints of interested persons within and without the university (including views expressed by the managements of portfolio companies), obtain the opinion of the university's investment managers concerning the economic impact of any exercise of shareholder rights, and, finally, render a report and recommendation to the trustees.

Although the responsibility for decision would rest with the board of trustees, it would be asked to indulge a presumption in favor of the council's recommendations; it would be expected to reject them where the council had departed from the criteria established by the Guidelines or had made factual findings not supported by the available data.

Are these mechanisms and procedures overly elaborate and cumbersome? We do not think so when compared to the contortions through which an entire university goes when it finds itself in a state of siege because it is not prepared to respond promptly and thoughtfully to urgent moral concerns voiced by students or faculty; or when compared to the burdens and complications imposed on the trustees if, for want of other channels, they have to serve as the initial clearinghouse for all grievances and communications; or when compared to the stresses and strains that would result if the trustees or any other component of the university had to make controversial decisions, under corporate deadlines, without established methods for obtaining data or for giving interested persons a timely opportunity to be heard.

It is in this procedural realm—and also with respect to jurisdictional criteria (indicating what kinds of corporate issues should produce what kinds of university response)—that our Guidelines are quite specific. Their detailed nature, however, may lead some institutional shareholders to assume, on first glance, that the Guidelines are equally specific on substantive matters—i.e., that they provide a detailed code for evaluation of corporate conduct, a "computer model" permitting easy resolution of social injury questions. A closer reading will reveal that we have not written such a substantive code; nor do we think we could have drafted a set of normative criteria that would have anticipated and dealt thoughtfully with the vast variety of social questions that confront a corporation over a period of years in a world of rapid change. Yet we hope that the Guidelines, by offering a principle for decision (the social injury test) and by referring the decision-maker to norms established by public bodies, will assist the university to begin the process of developing its own set of precedents to guide future decisions.

In proposing a fairly circumscribed set of criteria to guide the exercise of university investment responsibility, we have been largely influenced, of course, by the necessity of preserving a climate conducive to teaching and scholarship—a climate we have called the *Academic Context*. We have been influenced also by the difficulty of trying to write guidelines that go beyond the domain of "negative injunction" into the thicket of "affirmative duty."

As we note in chapter 3, there are institutions of higher learning for which the maintenance of the Academic Context must coexist with the implementation of certain social-moral values rooted in the religious or other ideological origins of the school. These colleges or universities may well find it appropriate to try to do more than apply self-governing negative injunctions to their investment activities.

But whether or not these schools opt for such affirmative action, they and all other institutions of higher learning can properly adopt the minimum approach to investment responsibility reflected in our proposed guidelines. And although this study does not focus on institutional investors other than universities, we take the liberty of suggesting that *all* charitable organizations could reasonably implement these policies as a baseline approach, even though many charities will find it possible or even essential to assume a more active posture. Indeed, because these Guidelines are meant to express the minimum moral obligation to which all individuals and institutions are subject, we think it appropriate for *non*charitable investors—pension funds, mutual funds, insurance companies, etc.—to consider the adoption of these Guidelines, modifying the procedures, of course, to fit the organizational format.

Even though these negative injunction Guidelines will represent, for some institutions, only a minimum or baseline approach, the investors which follow them will find that there is quite a bit for them to do. The very act of deciding to police investment and shareholder activity to avoid participation in social injury will represent a substantial, controversial, and perhaps painful increment of institutional change for many boards of trustees. And, having taken that step, it will not be easy to make the case-by-case decisions our proposed Guidelines call for; a look at the hypothetical cases set forth in chapter 4 will suggest some of the analytical and judgmental difficulties.

In short, if colleges and universities (or other institutional investors) set about the business of self-regulation, they will have challenging work to perform. And we are persuaded that it will be important work. The application of negative injunctions, to be sure, will not rebuild cities or make deserts bloom, but it can limit or halt the destruction of life, of opportunity, and of beauty. That may not be enough, but it is a great deal.

2. The Responsibilities of Corporations and Their Owners

For better or worse, the modern American business corporation is increasingly being asked to assume more responsibility for social problems and the public welfare. How corporate responsibility is understood, and whether it is perceived to be for better or worse, may depend in the last analysis on the beholder's emotional reaction to the corporation itself: one either extols the corporation as part of the creative process or condemns it as the work of the Devil. Thus, almost four centuries ago the English jurist Sir Edward Coke wrote of corporations that "they cannot commit treason nor be outlawed nor excommunicated for they have no souls," while more recently Justice Louis D. Brandeis characterized the corporation as the "master instrument of civilized life."[1]

We do not attempt to resolve all the controversy surrounding the notion of corporate responsibility, let alone to pronounce judgment on the state (if any) of the corporate soul. We do not, for example, investigate in any depth questions which have to do with the power and size of corporations, their relationship to the other institutions of our society, and their history in legal and constitutional thought.[2] But in order to examine institutional investor choices, we must at least outline the various ways in which corporate responsibility can be understood. And these differing views of corporate responsibility can best be analyzed if we start with a look at social responsibility in general terms.

First then, we will deal with some themes and problems surrounding the notion of the social responsibility of all individuals. Next, we will apply this discussion to the business corporation, and then to the role of the stockholder in relation to the social responsibility of corporations.

A GENERAL VIEW OF RESPONSIBILITY

Our analysis of the controversies surrounding the notion of cor-

porate responsibility—and the suggestion that the university as an
investor should be concerned with corporate responsibility—proceeds in large part from our approach to certain issues in the area
of social responsibility and public morals. In particular, we
(1) make a distinction between negative injunctions and affirmative duties; (2) assert that all men have the "moral minimum"
obligation not to impose social injury; (3) delineate those conditions under which one is held responsible for social injury, even
where it is not clear that the injury was self-caused; and (4) take a
position in the argument between those who strive for moral
purity and those who strive for moral effectiveness.

Negative Injunctions and Affirmative Duties

A distinction which informs much of our discussion differentiates
between injunctions against activities that injure others and duties
which require the affirmative pursuit of some good. The failure to
make this distinction in debate on public ethics often results in
false dichotomies, a point illustrated by an article which appeared
just over a decade ago in the *Harvard Business Review*. In that
article, which provoked considerable debate in the business community, Theodore Levitt argued against corporate social responsibility both because it was dangerous for society and because it
detracted from the primary goal of business, the making of profit.
We deal with the merits of these arguments later; what is important for our immediate purpose, however, is Levitt's designation
of those activities and concerns which constitute social responsibility. He notes that the corporation has become "more concerned about the needs of its employees, about schools, hospitals,
welfare agencies and even aesthetics," and that it is "fashion-
able ... for the corporation to show that it is a great innovator;
more specifically, a great public benefactor; and, very particularly, that it exists 'to serve the public'."[3] Having so delimited the
notion of corporate responsibility, Levitt presents the reader with
a choice between, on the one hand, getting involved in the management of society, "creating munificence for one and all," and,
on the other hand, fulfilling the profit-making function. But such
a choice excludes another meaning of corporate responsibility:

the making of profits in such a way as to minimize social injury. Levitt at no point considers the possibility that business activity may at times injure others and that it may be necessary to regulate the social consequences of one's business activities accordingly.

Levitt is certainly not alone in this approach to corporate responsibility.[4] The issue of responsible investing by universities has frequently been raised in much the same way: should university investments be oriented in a manner that will produce social good, i.e., ought universities to use their financial resources to attack some of society's more difficult problems? Thus posed, the question forces one to choose between devoting resources and energy to education and devoting resources and energy to doing good in noneducational ways. Faced with such a choice, the argument in favor of concentrating on education and letting others do good in other ways would be strong indeed. But this choice we are asked to make is a contrived necessity. It suggests that the only moral investment decision a university has to make concerns the amount of good it can achieve through investment action, thereby ignoring any duty it might have to avoid social harm in the pursuit of financial return. The question of avoiding social injury as a corporate investor thus bypassed, we are given the unhappy choice between education and charity.

Our public discourse abounds with similar failures to distinguish between positive and perhaps lofty ideals and minimal requirements of social organization. During the election campaigns of the 1950's and the civil rights movement of the early 1960's, the slogan, "You can't legislate morality," was a popular cry on many fronts. Obviously, we have not succeeded in devising laws that create within our citizens a predisposition to love and kindness; but we can devise laws which will minimize the injury that one citizen must suffer at the hands of another. Although the virtue of love may be the possession of a few, justice—in the minimal sense of not injuring others—can be required of all.

The distinction between negative injunctions and affirmative duties is old, having roots in common law and equity jurisprudence.[5] Here it is based on the premise that it is easier to specify and enjoin a civil wrong than to state what should be done. In the Ten Commandments, affirmative duties are spelled out only for one's relations with God and parents; for the more public relationships, we are given only the negative injunction: "Thou shalt not . . . ." Similarly, the Bill of Rights contains only negative injunctions.

Avoidance and Correction of Social Injury as a "Moral Minimum"

We do not mean to distinguish between negative injunctions and affirmative duties solely in the interests of analytical precision. The negative injunction to avoid and correct social injury threads its way through all morality. We call it a "moral minimum," implying that however one may choose to limit the concept of social responsibility, one cannot exclude this negative injunction. Although reasons may exist why certain persons or institutions cannot or should not be required to pursue moral or social good in all situations, there are many fewer reasons why one should be excused from the injunction against injuring others. Any citizen, individual or institutional, may have competing obligations which could, under some circumstances, override this negative injunction. But these special circumstances do not wipe away the prima facie obligation to avoid harming others.

In emphasizing the central role of the negative injunction, we do not suggest that affirmative duties are never important. A society where citizens go well beyond the requirement to avoid damage to others will surely be a better community. But we do recognize that individuals exhibit varying degrees of commitment to promote affirmatively the public welfare,* whereas we expect everyone equally to refrain from injuring others.

The view that all citizens are equally obligated to avoid or correct any social injury which is self-caused finds support in our legal as well as our moral tradition. H. L. A. Hart and A. M. Honoré have written:

---

*Because affirmative duties do not apply equally to all, our use of the term *duty* in this phrase is ambiguous. A more accurate, if more cumbersome, expression would be "the sometime duty to take affirmative social welfare action."

"Generally comprehensive and incisive, but with an excessively negative tone over-all, wouldn't you say?"

Drawing by D. Reilly; © 1971 The New Yorker Magazine, Inc.

In the moral judgments of ordinary life, we have occasion to blame people because they have caused harm to others, and also, if less frequently, to insist that morally they are bound to compensate those to whom they have caused harm. These are the moral analogues of more precise legal conceptions: for, in all legal systems liability to be punished or to make compensation frequently depends on whether actions (or omissions) have caused harm. Moral blame is not of course confined to such cases of causing harm.[6]

We know of no societies, from the literature of anthropology or comparative ethics, whose moral codes do not contain some injunction against harming others. The specific notion of *harm* or *social injury* may vary, as well as the mode of correction and restitution, but the injunctions are present.

In using the term *moral minimum* to describe this obligation, we mean to avoid any suggestion that the injunction against doing injury to others can serve as the basis for deriving the full content of morality. Moreover, we have used an expression which does not imply that the injunction is in any way dependent upon a natural law point of view. A person who subscribed to some form of natural law theory might indeed agree with our position, but so could someone who maintained that all morality is based on convention, agreement, or contract. Social contract theorists have generally maintained that the granting of rights to individuals by mutual consent involves some limitation on the actions of all individuals in the contract: to guarantee the liberty of all members, it is essential that each be enjoined against violating the rights of others.[7]

We asserted earlier that it is easier to enjoin and correct a wrong than it is to prescribe affirmatively what is good for society and what ought to be done. Notions of the public good and the values that men actively seek to implement are subjects of intense disagreement. In this realm, pluralism is almost inevitable, and some would argue that it is healthy. Yet there can also be disagreement about what constitutes social injury or harm. What some people think are affirmative duties may be seen by others as correction of social injury. For example, the notion that business corpora-tions should make special effort to train and employ members of minority groups could be understood by some to fulfill an affir-mative duty on the part of corporations to meet society's prob-lems; but it could be interpreted by others as the correction of a social injury caused by years of institutional racism. As a more extreme example, a Marxist would in all probability contend that *all* corporate activity is socially injurious and that therefore all social pursuits by corporations are corrective responses rather than affirmative actions.[8]

Although the notion of *social injury* is imprecise and although many hard cases will be encountered in applying it, we think that it is a helpful designation and that cases can be decided on the basis of it. In the law, many notions (such as *negligence* in the law of torts or *consideration* in the law of contracts) are equally vague but have received content from repeated decision-making over time. We would hope that under our proposed Guidelines similar "case law" would develop. Moreover, our Guidelines attempt to give some content to the notion of *social injury* by referring to external norms: *social injury* is defined as "particu-larly including activities which violate, or frustrate the enforce-ment of, rules of domestic or international law intended to pro-tect individuals against deprivation of health, safety or basic freedoms."[9]

In sum, we would affirm the prima facie obligation of all citi-zens, both individual and institutional, to avoid and correct self-caused social injury. Much more in the way of affirmative acts may be expected of certain kinds of citizens, but none is exempt from this "moral minimum."

In some cases it may not be true—or at least it may not be clear—that one has caused or helped to cause social injury, and yet one may bear responsibility for correcting or averting the injury. We consider next the circumstances under which this responsibility may arise.

Need, Proximity, Capability, and Last Resort
(The Kew Gardens Principle)

Several years ago the public was shocked by the news accounts of the stabbing and agonizingly slow death of Kitty Genovese in the Kew Gardens section of New York City while thirty-eight people watched or heard and did nothing.[10] What so deeply disturbed the public's moral sensibilities was that in the face of a critical human need, people who were close to that need and had the power to do something about it failed to act.

The public's reaction suggests that, no matter how narrowly one may conceive of social responsibility, there are some situations in which a combination of circumstances thrusts upon us an obligation to respond. Life is fraught with emergency situations in which a failure to respond is a special form of violation of the negative injunction against causing social injury: a sin of omission becomes a sin of commission.

Legal responsibility for aiding someone in cases of grave distress or injury, even when caused by another, is recognized by many European civil codes and by the criminal laws of one of our states:

> (A) A person who knows that another is exposed to grave physical harm shall, to the extent that the same can be rendered without danger or peril to himself or without interference with important duties owed to others, give reasonable assistance to the exposed person unless that assistance or care is being provided by others. . . .
>
> (C) A person who wilfully violates subsection (A) of this section shall be fined not more than $100.00.[11]

This Vermont statute recognizes that it is not reasonable in all cases to require a person to give assistance to someone who is endangered. If such aid imperils himself, or interferes with duties owed to others, or if there are others providing the aid, the person is excepted from the obligation. These conditions of responsibility give some shape to difficult cases and are in striking parallel with the conditions which existed at Kew Gardens. The salient features of the Kitty Genovese case are (1) critical need; (2) the proximity of the thirty-eight spectators; (3) the capability of the spectators to act helpfully (at least to telephone the police); and (4) the absence of other (including official) help; i.e., the thirty-eight were the last resort. There would, we believe, be widespread agreement that a moral obligation to aid another arises when these four features are present. What we have called the "moral minimum" (the duty to avoid and correct self-caused social injury) is an obvious and easy example of fulfillment of these criteria—so obvious that there is little need to go through step-by-step analysis of these factors. Where the injury is not clearly self-caused, the application of these criteria aids in deciding responsibility. We have called this combination of features governing difficult cases the "Kew Gardens Principle." There follows a more detailed examination of each of the features:

Need. In cases where the other three criteria are constant, increased need increases responsibility. Just as there is no precise definition of social injury (one kind of need), there is no precise definition of need or way of measuring its extent.

Proximity. The thirty-eight witnesses of the Genovese slaying were geographically close to the deed. But proximity to a situation of need is not necessarily spatial. Proximity is largely a function of notice: we hold a person blameworthy if he knows of imperilment and does not do what he reasonably can do to remedy the situation. Thus, the thirty-eight at Kew Gardens were delinquent not because they were near but because nearness enabled them to know that someone was in need. A deaf person who could not hear the cries for help would not be considered blameworthy even if he were closer than those who could hear. So also, a man in Afghanistan is uniquely responsible for the serious illness of a man in Peoria, Illinois, if he has knowledge of the man's illness, if he can telephone a doctor about it, and if he alone has that notice. When we become aware of a wrongdoing or a social injury, we take on obligations that we did not have while ignorant.

Notice does not exhaust the meaning of proximity, however. It

24 The Ethical Investor

is reasonable to maintain that the sick man's neighbors in Peoria were to some extent blameworthy if they made no effort to inquire into the man's welfare. Ignorance cannot always be helped, but we do expect certain persons and perhaps institutions to look harder for information about critical need.[12] In this sense, proximity has to do with the network of social expectations that flow from notions of civic duty, duties to one's family, and so on. Thus, we expect a man to be more alert to the plight of his next-door neighbor than to the needs of a child in East Pakistan, just as we expect a man to be more alert to the situation of his own children than to the problems of the family down the block. The failure of the man to act in conformance with this expectation does not give him actual notice of need, but it creates what the law would call *constructive notice*. Both factors—actual notice and constructive notice growing out of social expectation—enter into the determination of responsibility and blame.

Capability. Even if there is a need to which a person has proximity, that person is not usually held responsible unless there is something he can reasonably be expected to do to meet the need. To follow Immanuel Kant, *ought* assumes *can*. What one is reasonably capable of doing, of course, admits to some variety of interpretation. In the Kew Gardens incident, it might not have been reasonable to expect someone to place his body between the girl and the knife. It was surely reasonable to expect someone to call the police. So also it would not seem to be within the canons of reasonability for a university to sacrifice education for charity (the contrived choice mentioned earlier). But if the university is able, by non-self-sacrificial means, to mitigate injury caused by a company of which it is an owner, it would not seem unreasonable to ask it to do so.

Last Resort. In the emergency situations we have been describing, one becomes more responsible the less likely it is that someone else will be able to aid. Physical proximity is a factor here, as is time. If the knife is drawn, one cannot wait for the policeman. It is important to note here that determination of last resort becomes more difficult the more complex the social situation or organization. The man on the road to Jericho, in spite of the presence of a few other travelers, probably had a fairly good notion that he was the only person who could help the man attacked by thieves. But on a street in New York City, there is always the hope that someone else will step forward to give aid. Surely this rationalization entered into the silence of each of the thirty-eight: there were, after all, thirty-seven others. Similarly, within large corporations it is difficult to know not only whether one alone has notice of a wrongdoing, but also whether there is anyone else who is able to respond. Because of this diffusion of responsibility in complex organizations and societies, the notion of last resort is less useful than the other Kew Gardens criteria in determining whether one ought to act in aid of someone in need or to avert or correct social injury. Failure to act because one hopes someone else will act—or because one is trying to find out who is the last resort—may frequently lead to a situation in which no one acts at all.[13] This fact, we think, places more weight on the first three features of the Kew Gardens Principle in determining responsibility, and it creates a presumption in favor of taking action when those three conditions are present.[14]

Purity vs. Effectiveness

The question whether one ought to seek moral purity or moral effectiveness in public action arises in the context of investment policy: should a university or other investor sell the stock of a company whose policies it finds morally abhorrent, or should it retain its shares and attempt to change the policies of that company? To some extent, this choice reflects the difference between the Kantians and the Utilitarians, between those who judge the goodness of an act on the basis of its conformity to principle and those who judge the goodness of an act according to its effect.

It will surely appear to the reader of chapter 3 and the Guidelines that we have sided with those who look to moral effect. It is true that we have taken seriously the effect of moral actions, but we doubt that the two types of ethical appeal are genuinely separable. The debate on this issue is ancient and intricate. Suffice it to say here that, in the realm of personal morality, one may abstain from certain acts not only because of their own impact, but also because such regular abstention steels the character for future cases where an immoral act will be harder to resist—and even more injurious.[15] Whether there is an institutional equivalent of character is surely debatable, and therefore the "steeling" argument may not apply to institutions. But either for the purpose of "steeling" or because of some lingering notion of purity, we believe that when an institution has made every attempt to modify certain corporate policies and has not succeeded, there is merit in dissolving ties with the corporation in order to prevent being locked in to a policy that is morally repugnant. Moreover, although it is impossible to gauge the symbolic effect of apparently insignificant gestures, the dissolution of ties with a corporation when all else has failed may also represent a last-ditch effort to avert social harm. (See pp. 92-93.)

Any quest for moral purity alone, however, seems hopelessly naive. To attempt to cleanse one's portfolio of dirty stocks and to invest only in clean stocks would involve one in an endless series of illusions and arbitrary decisions. We share George Bernard Shaw's point of view reflected in his comment on the clergyman who would accept money only from sweet old ladies:

> He has only to follow up the income of the sweet ladies to its industrial source, and there he will find Mrs. Warren's profession and the poisonous canned meat and all the rest of it. His own stipend has the same root. He must either share the world's guilt or go to another planet.[16]

Too many people, however, let the matter rest here: because one cannot avoid contamination, one cannot do anything at all. The complex organization and inter-relatedness of the world is invoked in either existentialist despair or bureaucratic indifference, and the guilt of all becomes the guilt of no one. This result is unacceptable. We may not be able to avoid the world's guilt, but we can seek to reduce the level of injury. That no course of action is untainted does not mean that no course of action is preferable to another or that we cannot choose between more and less desirable consequences.

CORPORATIONS AND SOCIAL RESPONSIBILITY

From the conclusion that all citizens, individual and institutional, are equally subject to the negative injunction against social injury, it follows that there is a prima facie obligation on the part of business corporations to regulate their activities so that they do not injure others and so that they correct what injury they do cause. Our task in this section is to consider whether this prima facie obligation is swept aside by the most frequently stated objections to the notion of corporate responsibility. We intend also to indicate in a tentative way how more affirmative notions of corporate responsibility are affected by the objections.

Before moving to the objections, it will be helpful to sort out the various meanings of the phrase *corporate responsibility*. It can be and has been applied to four different but often overlapping categories of corporate behavior: (1) self-regulation in the avoidance of social injury (the negative injunction); or, on the other end of the spectrum, (2) the championing of political and moral causes unrelated to the corporation's business activities, perhaps including some gifts of charity. Somewhere on the continuum between these poles (but sharing some aspects of each) lies (3) affirmative action extending beyond self-regulation but falling short of the championing of causes—for example, cooperation with government in training hard-core unemployed, or the use of corporate resources (including manpower and facilities) in response to certain needs or social problems in the corporation's home community. Corporate responsibility also sometimes refers to (4) internal reforms and changes in corporate structure which will affect the voting rights of shareholders, or the prerogatives of management (increasing or decreasing its power), or the flow of information between these groups and other corporate constituencies.

In some cases, corporate responsibility concepts can be expressed in economic terms. Thus, what we have called the avoidance and correction of social injury is often a matter of a corporation internalizing costs which have been externalized or imposed on the larger society.[17] Although we are not sure that all social injury can be understood as the externalization of costs (discrimination against Blacks in hiring is not really an externalized cost of doing business), this language often aids discussion of the issues, especially since some of the objections to notions of corporate responsibility are based on economic considerations.

The most important objections to the proposition that a corporation should concern itself with moral and social issues seem to be the following: (1) Competing claims: A corporation cannot undertake socially oriented action without impairing its contribution to the economic health of society. (2) Competitive disadvantage: It is unfair to ask corporations to deal with social issues because such activity puts the corporation at a competitive disadvantage. (3) Competence: The corporation is not competent to deal with social and moral issues. (4) Fairness: Corporate action on social and moral issues will coerce other persons and institutions and thus necessarily fails to meet minimal standards of fairness. (5) Legitimacy: Only government can legitimately deal with the prevention and correction of social and moral problems. Although the considerations under each of the five headings overlap at many points, these categories serve to give focus to the most important issues.

Competing Claims

The issue presented here is part of a general question about whether the corporation is capable of taking responsibility for social problems. Clear positions have been taken on both sides of the question. One of the strongest affirmative answers was given by George Champion of the Chase Manhattan Bank in a speech a few years ago:

> All of us are familiar with the vital spark that the competitive factor has provided in our economic development. . . .
>
> Just imagine what could be accomplished if some of this competitive zest were channeled into public service. Think of the good that could be done if business were to launch an all-out campaign of creative competition with government in developing imaginative new approaches to economic and social problems.

What I am suggesting is that business might compete with government by setting up projects that would represent beachheads of excellence throughout the country. These would be in the nature of pilot programs in social experimentation that could serve as models for others in the future. By establishing standards of quality and cost for the government to emulate, these public-service projects would exert a cumulative effect far greater than their immediate impact.[18]

And a recent statement published by the Committee for Economic Development asserts:

Business enterprises have demonstrated many of the qualities and capabilities that appear to be critically needed in the solution of many of the country's social problems. They often possess comparative advantages over other institutions as respects innovation; technological competence; organizational training and managerial abilities; and certain performance characteristics and disciplines.[19]

One could easily find other examples of the belief that corporations are uniquely qualified to meet some of the current pressing social problems.

Almost as common, however, is the negative response focusing on those characteristics of a corporation which, it is said, uniquely disqualify it from taking responsibility for social and moral problems. In his article cited earlier, Theodore Levitt contends, first, that the notion of corporate responsibility is dangerous for society (see "Fairness," p. 39, for further discussion on this point), and second, that consideration of social issues has a debilitating effect on the business function of the corporation:

. . . if something does not make economic sense, sentiment or idealism ought not to let it in the door. Sentiment is a corrupting and debilitating influence in business. It fosters leniency, inefficiency, sluggishness, extravagance, and hardens the innovating arteries. . . .

Business will have a much better chance of surviving if there is no nonsense about its goals—that is, if long-run profit maximization is the one dominant objective in practice as well as in theory.[20]

In a similar vein, Milton Friedman has argued that corporate executives are "incredibly shortsighted and muddle-headed in matters that are outside their business but affect the possible survival of business in general" and that consequently any attempt on the part of corporate executives to attend to noneconomic questions will of necessity diffuse the energies of business, foster inefficiency, and undermine the health of the economic system as a whole.[21]

Essentially, the Levitt-Friedman position makes two points regarding the capability of corporations to assume social responsibility: undertaking any activity which is not oriented toward maximizing profit will undermine the efficiency of the corporation, preventing it from fulfilling its chief responsibility to society as a whole; and, in addition, corporations will do damage to society by working in areas in which they are not competent. We deal with the competence issue under a separate heading, below. Here, we treat the question of the competing claim of efficiency.

The general argument is that consideration of any factors other than profit-maximizing ones either results in a deliberate sacrifice of profits or muddies the process of corporate decision-making so as to impair profitability. Consequently, resources will not be put to the highest use dictated by a free-market system, and the total sum of economic resources available for meeting social problems (available, for example, to be taxed and channeled through public efforts to meet social needs or available as direct benefits in terms of goods and services) will be critically reduced. In addition, those who are investing in a corporation or any others trying to judge the performance of that corporation will have no solid criteria for evaluation. This last contention—if it refers to anything other than measuring convenience—must take us back to the premise that the only reliable gauge of a corporation's performance is its profitability. Thus, Eugene Rostow writes that "I, for one, conclude that a clear-cut economic directive should help directors to discriminate more effectively among competing claims upon them, in carrying out their public trusteeship for the economic system as a whole."[22]

There are, it seems to us, four not entirely separable problems with the profit-maximizing imperative (not all of which are applicable to each of the authors we have quoted): it tends to emphasize the profits of an individual firm rather than the profits of the corporate sector as a whole; it sometimes tends to emphasize short-term rather than long-term profit; it neglects aspects of corporate "well-being" other than profit; it assumes that profit is a true measure of the capacity of a business institution to contribute efficiently to the total material wealth of the society.

Individual Firm vs. Corporate Sector. In a recent analysis of the implications for the shareholder of corporate involvement in social problems, Henry C. Wallich and John J. McGowan distinguish among three "possible investment bases that a corporation might adopt":

> The *narrowest* base would take account only of returns directly appropriable by the corporation. . . . An *intermediate* policy would include returns appropriable through the market system by the corporate sector as a whole [such as "investment in manpower training . . . worthwhile for the industry as a whole"] . Finally, a *wide-based* approach . . . would include not only market-appropriable returns but also returns accruing to the community (including corporations and stockholders) not appropriable through the market by the corporate sector.[23]

The *narrow-based* approach, the authors observe, will permit corporations as a whole to earn less on their invested capital than the intermediate approach—an approach which "would lead corporations to assume a substantial role in social policy. . . ."[24] In other words, certain forms of "corporate involvement in social policy" which may not maximize returns for a single firm may nevertheless benefit "firms as a group."[25] This analysis, combined with the assumption that corporations are owned "by individuals who as a group typically own shares in a very large number of corporations," lead the authors to state that although the *wide-based* approach may or may not benefit shareholders, the *intermediate* approach will benefit shareholders more than the *narrowest* approach.[26] "The conclusion of this analysis is that the proposition that corporate involvement in social policy is contrary to the shareholders' interest is both misleading and irrelevant."[27] The Research and Policy Committee of the Committee for Economic Development summed up the point this way:

> Stockholders' interests, therefore, tend to ride with corporations as a group and with investment policies which provide benefits to the corporate sector as a whole—in the form of improved environmental conditions, a better labor force, and stronger public approval of private business. That is, corporations as a group—and singly as well, under reasonable assumptions—will earn more on their invested capital, and stockholders will be better off if these broader investment policies are adopted.[28]

Short Term vs. Long Term. Many corporate managers argue that, even for the individual firm, it is *profitable* to pursue certain social goals, especially if one takes into account long-term considerations (Champion's statement, quoted earlier, implies that this is a possibility). This contention may be stated in the negative: a firm cannot assure profitability in the future unless it protects the safety of the entire environment through whatever means are necessary. As Donald Schwartz has pointed out, ". . . isn't the mark of the highly intelligent manager his sense of proportion? The corporate enterprise will outlast him and its present shareholders. If it is to survive into the next generation it will require the acceptance of the society in which it lives, and of course, that society must live. So, it is shortsighted, and ultimately unproductive, to ignore the effect of what he is doing on the community around him."[29]

Although Levitt and Friedman may question the capacity of business managers to implement this approach, the law has clearly recognized the manager's right to do so. Phillip Blumberg, summarizing the development of the law on this point, has noted that "even though the activity may have no immediate profit-orientation, it still may well represent a business-oriented decision to advance the long-term position and interests of the corporation, with the expenditure regarded as a politically inevitable cost of doing business."[30]

In a related vein, it is sometimes contended that some expenditures designed to improve a company's social performance may save money by anticipating future government requirements or public demands.[31] It may be cheaper, for example, to incorporate pollution control equipment into a plant when it is first constructed than to revamp the facility at a later date in response to legal or other constraints. Here, again, the short-term and long-term prognoses may be rather different.

We pause to point out that people will not always agree on what will be profitable in the immediate future for an individual firm. For example, Clem Morgello, writing in *Newsweek,* asks, "If the [SST] program is revived, how many General Electric stockholders would vote that the company *not* produce the SST engine because the plane might seriously damage the environment"—implying that loss of the SST contract would create a profit loss.[32] But a research bulletin published by a well-known investment management firm announced that cancellation of the SST would "have little impact on General Electric's earnings" and "could be slightly positive for short-term earnings."[33]

No matter how broad the definition of *profitability,* it cannot be argued that *all* corporate measures *pro bono publico,* including what we have called affirmative action and charity, can be deemed ultimately profitable ("What is good for the country is good for General Motors"). It is true that, for legal or stockholder-relations reasons, corporate managers attempt to justify much of what they do, not on the merits of the act itself but in terms of profit. Thus, Adolf Berle has written:

The fact is that boards of directors or corporation executives are often faced with situations in which quite humanly and simply they consider that such and such is the decent thing to do and ought to be done. . . . They apply the potential profits or public relation tests later on, a sort of left-handed justification in this curious free-market world where an obviously moral or decent or humane action has to be apologized for on the ground that conceivably, you may somehow make money by it.[34]

Although in some cases a socially responsible act may also be a profitable act, a complete congruence between profit and responsibility cannot be assumed.[35]

In sum, the pursuit of social goals may enhance profits sufficiently to cast doubt on the efficiency objection to corporate responsibility. But the relationship is not clear enough to constitute an independent rationale for corporate responsibility.

Other Indicators of Well-being. Uncertainty about what will be profitable—either in the short or the long run—constitutes at least one of the reasons why managers look to indicators other than profit-maximization to judge corporate performance and well being. As Richard Eells has pointed out, " . . . 'buying cheap and selling dear' does not describe the profit goal of most large industrial corporations today. When businessmen define their goal as not maximization of profit but rather the avoidance of loss, the assurance of a 'required minimum profit' to cover future risks, to attract equity capital, and to guarantee corporate survival, we are obviously in the presence of ends to which profitability may seem to be secondary."[36]

In addition to the corporate goals listed by Eells, many managers would list long-term growth and equitable distribution of corporate gain as high on their list of objectives.[37] This shift in managerial thinking about corporate goals has occasioned suggestions that we need either to redefine the function of the corporation as something other than profit-making,[38] or to redefine *profit.* For example, Daniel Lufkin has called for a "redefinition, not an abolition of the concept of profit—one that will assess corporate gains and losses, not only in terms of dollars but also in terms of social benefits realized."[39]

We do not suggest that profit is no indicator at all of corporate well-being, or even that it is not the chief indicator (it may or may not be); we do suggest that complete agreement has not been reached on what will be profitable, and that the indicators of corporate well being are at best ambiguous and not confined to either short-term or long-term profit. From these two points, we may also conclude that when a corporation considers social factors in its business decisions, the resulting difficulty for the public in assessing its performance or effectiveness is nothing new; that difficulty has always existed for the thoughtful corporation-watcher.

Efficient Use of National Resources. Finally, we turn to the assumption that profitability—even if we could always gauge it and even if it were the only indicator of corporate health—measures the capacity of the company to contribute efficiently to society's material prosperity. The difficulties with this position are most easily seen in examining the case for the negative injunction against corporate social injury. If the highest profit is gained from a business activity which, at the same time, imposes social injury—if it ravishes the environment or discriminates against minority groups—then profit-maximization has produced a countervailing inefficiency in the use of natural and human resources. In these cases, the argument for efficient allocation of resources would appear to require the corporation to locate and regulate the social consequences of its own conduct.

As we have already noted, social injury is, in many cases, a matter of a company's externalizing its costs. By asking corporations to internalize some of these costs—that is, to prevent and correct social injury—we are suggesting that some of the costs imposed on society are either disproportionate to the benefits gained in the production of goods or services and/or of a kind that the larger society ought not to be asked to absorb. Not all costs should necessarily be internalized, however: some might better be handled through taxation in order to avoid the regressive impact of passing on to consumers the so-called internalized costs. For example, increased prices of basic necessities due to correction of social injury would place a disproportionate burden on the poor. In any event, there is no apparent reason to accept as axiomatic that unregulated profit-maximization will contribute to the most efficient or wisest use of all resources.

There are, in fact, many persons who suggest that the opposite is true. In a recent article, J. Irwin Miller has argued that we need to face directly the probability that the solutions to many of contemporary society's critical needs will require us to choose between those solutions and profitability, and to reorder our priorities in the market system, even to the extent of accepting a cutback in the private standard of living.[40]

Even were this not the case, however—even if the resource-efficiency point we have been rebutting were invulnerable—the negative injunction against social injury would have to be respected. Thus, for example, even if one could not prove that a particular injury constituted a "countervailing inefficiency," it would be difficult to argue that this injury should be ignored in order to pursue a profit-maximizing policy. It is possible that Friedman (and others who share his approach) would not disagree here.[41] But most of the debate on corporate responsibility, by rather carelessly focusing on what we have termed *affirmative duties* rather than the *negative injunctions* and by raising efficiency to the level of the highest virtue, has obscured what seems to be the fundamental point: that economic activity, like any human activity, can have unwanted and injurious side-effects, and that the correction of these indirect consequences requires self-regulation. This is the meaning for the business corporation of what we have called the "moral minimum"—the negative injunction to avoid social injury—which cannot be set aside where there are reasonable ways to obey it.[42]

Competitive Disadvantage

On the assumption that good works will not always be profitable but may indeed cost money, it is sometimes contended that any corporation taking on good works will be at a competitive disadvantage in the market.[43] For this reason, it is argued, all such responsible activity must be either carried on by the government or at least regulated by government so that all corporations or industries will be subject to the same requirements. (We shall deal later with the larger question of the government's proper role.)

Insofar as social injury is caused by a particular corporation and not by its industry peers this argument has little force. For example, if the company discriminates in hiring and claims that the only way it can remain competitive is through continued discrimination, that is the company's problem and no one else's. There is no reason why a corporation should remain in business if it can prosper only by inflicting social harm. *Case*

If the injury occasioned is unique not to the corporation itself but rather to an industry (e.g., a pollution problem peculiar to one industry), the individual corporation can at least be expected to work for industrywide self-regulation within the limits of anti- *Case* trust laws;[44] or, the individual firm can work for government regulation which would alleviate the problem without putting the company at a competitive disadvantage. On this point, the Research and Policy Committee of the Committee for Economic Development has recently stated:

> Indeed, if corporations cannot deal individually with major social responsibilities such as pollution because of competitive cost disadvantages, and if they are unable to cooperate in resolving such difficulties, then they logically and ethically should propose and support rational governmental regulation which will remove the short-run impediments from actions that are wise in the long run.[45]

It could be further contended that the correction of certain kinds of social injury would create insuperable technological problems for a corporation acting on its own—that in some cases government help might be needed to solve these problems and that to require the corporation to internalize these costs alone would be to impose an undue competitive penalty. But in such situations it does not seem unreasonable to require the corporation to request the needed government assistance.

Competence

Even accepting the premise that a corporation is capable of being socially responsible without unduly sacrificing resource efficiency or without being put at an unfair competitive disadvantage,) one may still claim that the corporation is incompetent to deal with social and moral issues and will therefore do more damage than good. Friedman suggests that businessmen are "muddleheaded" in this area. This claim could mean several different things and has several corresponding rejoinders.

First, the claim may mean that corporations have no technical skills to deal with social issues.[46] Surely, the accuracy of this contention varies from case to case. For example, some corporations are especially qualified technically to train hard-core unemployed (although the programs undertaken by corporations have yet to be pronounced successful); a company that produces antipollution devices may be most qualified to deal with certain pollution problems. Moreover, this objection is persuasive only if there is some other person or entity that can do the job better. This condition, too, will vary from case to case. Finally, this technical-skill objection seems inapplicable to corporate self-regulation: a company is in a reasonable position to perceive, and at least attempt to regulate, the social consequences of its own conduct. However, a corporation might be in a quandary about how to end or correct a social injury. For example, knowledge that a corporation's economic activity in a third-world nation has an undesirable effect on American foreign policy does not tell the corporation how to remedy that effect. And some problems cannot be solved without government help, both technical and financial.[47] But once more, in such situations the sensible thing to do is to ask for advice or assistance, either from government or other sources.

Second, the claim of incompetence may mean that corporations do not know what is good for society. (Again, this point seems to be aimed not at self-regulation but at more affirmative modes of action.) Corporations do not have privileged access to the nature of the good, and we are at least willing to entertain the suggestion that some other institution (e.g., government) is better equipped to set social goals. But a corporation's alleged lack of insight into the nature of the good is not a reason for *objecting* to its social activities unless they are deliberately coercive or, because of sheer size, inherently coercive, or so incompetent that they invite excessive government intervention—possibilities to be taken up shortly.

Finally, the claim may mean that incompetent attempts by corporations to contribute to the resolution of moral and social problems will ultimately result in the wasting of shareholders' money. To the extent that the managers and the shareholders are in agreement about the social program, wasting shareholders' money simply means that they did not achieve what they and the managers were both after—an effective social program. Thus, we are back to the general question of corporate competence. If, on the other hand, a given corporate management decides to pursue certain social goals according to its own predilections—which are not shared by the stockholders—such activity could be considered a waste of stockholder money, apart from the question of competence. In such cases, some protection for the shareholder in the use of his funds could be achieved by altering the decision-making process to permit shareholder voices to be heard on pertinent issues.[48] (We return to this topic, and to the related question of shareholder competence to deal with social issues, in the next section on "Shareholders and Corporate Responsibility.")

Fairness

The issue of fairness refers to the contention that corporate moral and social decisions will have coercive effect and that such coercion, operating without legal safeguards, may be arbitrary and unfair. Although this charge may be made about other actors, it has special force in the case of corporations because of their considerable size and power.

One of America's venerable traditions is apprehension of bigness in any form, especially Big Business. From this perspective, the movement toward corporate responsibility is no more than a cover-up for granting corporate managers even more discretionary power over the lives of others. Thus, one of Levitt's main thrusts is the danger inherent in corporate seeking of social ends:

> What we have . . . is the frightening spectacle of a powerful economic functional group whose future and perception are

shaped in a tight materialistic context of money and things but which imposes its narrow ideas about a broad spectrum of un-related non-economic subjects on the mass of men and society.

Even if its outlook were the purest kind of good will, that would not recommend the corporation as an arbiter of our lives. What is bad for this or any other country is for society to be consciously and aggressively shaped by a single ideology, whatever if may be.[49]

Leaving aside Levitt's characterization of corporations as "tight-ly materialistic," corporate weight-throwing is a problem. But the threat of bigness is frequently asserted with very little specific content, making it difficult to judge the implications of bigness for corporate responsibility.

What is the effect of corporate bigness? Essentially, its im-pact—apart from any commercial, anticompetitive conse-quences—is felt in three ways: (1) direct political activity; (2) governing of corporate employees; and (3) the indirect, smothering effect.

Political Action. Corporate political lobbying has become an accepted part of American political life especially on the national level and increasingly on the state and local levels.[50] Much of this lobbying seeks to advance the specific business interests of the corporations. But the larger the corporation and the more clout it has, the more this business lobbying is likely to affect areas be-yond business. This is most obvious when companies press for particular interests and concessions in international business, the consequences of which may affect American foreign policy. Furthermore, corporate political activity is not confined merely to lobbying. There is also direct support on the local and state levels for political candidates and parties,[51] as well as support of mass media programs which explore or take positions on political, social, and moral issues. In a variety of ways, then, large corpora-tions give direction to the political life of the country, the impact of which is not limited to the business world.

Private Government. A growing literature describes the corporation as a private government. There are those who maintain that the most tangible political structure that many men encounter in daily life is that of the corporation by which they are employed; and that as a "private government," it operates without the Constitutional safeguards imposed on public agencies.[52] Marquis W. Childs and Douglass Cater have written:

> But decisions taken by the mayor, the city council, the county manager, the governor of the state have comparatively little bearing on the daily life of the average citizen. It is his relation to the business for which he works that conditions his whole life. About this relationship he has little or nothing to say, particularly if he is one of the many millions of Americans who work for corporations employing a thousand or more workers.[53]

The Smothering Effect. Apart from direct political activity and internal governing processes, a large corporation can affect persons in the wider society simply by smothering everything around it, by closing off options. This phenomenon is perhaps most obvious on the local level: a large enterprise can support an entire city, limiting employment and consumer options and even determining the values, tastes, and life style of the community.[54] But on the national level, too, corporate bigness can affect the lives of persons by shaping consumer choices through advertising and product decisions, and by exercising some control of the flow of information through ownership of the mass media. Leonard Silk has noted that "in the past the essence of American business power has been ideological—that is, it has provided the value conceptions and set the limit upon what the nation is doing or trying to do."[55]

Assuming that these are some of the effects of Big Business in American life, what conclusions are we to draw for the future of corporate social responsibility? Levitt, Friedman, and others have concluded that corporate power will become more dangerous if the corporations enter nonbusiness areas. But if the foregoing assumption is correct—that corporations already have political, governing, and value-setting effects in nonbusiness areas—then the problem is not a new one. Moreover, if large corporations do have a Midas touch that turns all affirmative moral action into coercive erosion of freedom, this phenomenon must derive from the powers of bigness we have already discussed. If so, we need to find new ways to control, limit, or legitimize these considerable powers, rather than to imagine that they represent a problem only in the social policy context.

Turning to our self-regulatory approach, there is no reason to suppose that the attempt to understand and regulate the direct and indirect social effects of a company's own activities will be an imposition on others or subject them to arbitrary action. Indeed, *lack* of such self-regulation may be much more arbitrary in its effects. A company that decides for business reasons to move to a new location without attempting to regulate the socially injurious impacts of the move may find that it has perpetuated or reinforced patterns of discrimination and poverty. (See hypothetical case P, chapter 4.) We grant that even corporate self-regulation may have some spill-over effect—that the attempt to avoid or correct a self-caused social injury may have some influence on the freedom of action of others. Such effects will, we think, be relatively insignificant when compared to the benefits of self-correction.

While a program of self-regulation in the avoidance and correction of social injury seems to mitigate rather than aggravate the problems created by corporate bigness, we are far less sanguine about some of the more affirmative modes of corporate responsibility. The active championing of political and moral causes does seem to be a form of weight-throwing that may minimize the options of others. On the other hand, should we fault the attempts of corporate managements to respond to genuine human needs, to go some steps beyond the minimal requirements of law and negative injunctions? J. Irwin Miller recently wrote of corporate giving to the arts: "I find highly offensive the argument of a well-known economist that the business of business is to do business. You can call it a rule of thumb that where corporations do more than the law requires you have a good society."[56]

There is a difference between charitable gifts to the arts and the job training of minority group members, on the one hand, and the championing of a corporate point of view on moral or political questions, on the other. The second category may more readily involve a corporate attempt to impose values on others. But the line between the two categories, as between leadership and manipulation, is fine indeed. Whether an affirmative corporate social activity becomes an impingement upon personal freedom is a function of many factors: the number of people affected, whether those people requested the corporate response or had it handed to them, the amount of corporate resources involved, the nature of this issue. Questions of this sort need more explication than we can give here.

In sum, we are convinced that the type of corporate self-regulation we have proposed will help to limit the arbitrary and oppressive impact of corporate activity, rather than the opposite, and therefore does not present a fairness problem.

Legitimacy

Is the corporation, in undertaking social responsibilities, usurping the role of government? At least three positions, anticipated in the preceding discussion of other issues, are distinguishable.

First, it is frequently maintained that contemporary social problems are so acute that unless business steps in to solve them, the government will enter. In this view, corporate social involvement does not represent a problem for human freedom; on the contrary, the danger arises from a vacuum which will be filled by governmental encroachment on the private realm. Moreover, corporate social problem-solving is pluralistic and therefore preferable to the monolithic approach of the federal government. This is the position taken by George Champion:

> I can think of nothing that would put the brakes on Big Government faster than for business to identify critical problems and take the initiative in dealing with them before Washington felt the need to act. The polls have shown repeatedly that whenever people see a viable alternative to government action, they are likely to support it. They favor gov-

ernment intervention only when there seems to be no other way.[57]

Second, it is almost as frequently contended that if corporations deal with social problems, they will bungle so badly that government will have to undo the mess, thereby causing more encroachment on private activity from *both* business and government. This seems to be the position taken by Levitt, Friedman, and other writers.[58]

Both of the preceding positions want to minimize the role of government. A third position argues that only federal regulatory and economic subsidy programs can deal with the widespread disjunctions caused by imperfect markets, rapid and uneven growth of technology, and discriminatory practices. The judgment that only government can act effectively is based on at least two assumptions: (1) that the required remedies do involve some encroachment on human freedom (but no more than is present without the remedies) and thus should be carried out by publicly constituted authorities; and (2) that society, to function well, must have an orderly division of labor—with regulatory and economic subsidy programs the tasks of government.

These three positions clearly rest on very different judgments about the nature of public authority, the relation between business activity and the rest of society, and probably the doctrine of Original Sin. Although we cannot consider here all of these fundamental questions, we do offer several comments.

The positions outlined above have evolved in the context of asking who has the affirmative duty to solve society's problems. This is quite different from asking how one can attempt to regulate the social consequences of whatever activity one happens to be pursuing. Most of the views advanced about the respective roles of government and business have not addressed this area of negative injunctions.

It might nevertheless be argued that government is the proper regulator of the social consequences of business activity even in the negative injunction sense. Apart from the fact that we see little harm in duplication of effort (in having a complementary set of regulators—the corporations themselves), there is the consideration that the machinery of government doesn't always work. It has frequently been observed that the federal agencies that were created to regulate the various sectors of the corporate world often tend to represent industry interests rather than to limit and control them.[59] Grant McConnell has characterized this as a condition in which ". . . government is kept informed, but by the same token it is often made to be arbitrary. Decisions made under such conditions are responsible to power which can be welded over the official agency. The process amounts in some situations to the capture of government. However, it is not 'rule' as this is normally conceived; it is the fragmentation of rule and the conquest of pieces of governmental authority by different groups."[60] This perception of the regulatory process underlines the necessity of not counting on government to avert and correct social injury.

One could argue, of course, that energy ought to be directed at reforming the regulatory process. Such efforts are praiseworthy, but they do not obviate the duty to practice self-regulation.

Indeed, even if government regulation worked more efficiently, it is unlikely that it would handle all such problems. For example, much of the activity of large international corporations takes place outside the jurisdiction of the United States government. Although they may at times be subjected to the laws and regulations of other nations, the international corporations have a freedom not only from American federal control but also from the countervailing powers of labor unions and other forces in the American market which might limit their power. Karl Kaysen writes in this regard:

Another instance of the peculiar "privacy" of the large firm is the power in both domestic and foreign affairs which the large oil companies have by virtue of their special positions as concessionaries—frequently on a monopoly basis in a particular country—in exploiting the oil of the Middle East and the Caribbean. Here the large firms exercise quasi-sovereign powers, have large influence on certain aspects of the foreign policy of the United States and the Atlantic Alliance and operate in a way which is neither that of public government nor that of private business.[61]

American corporate involvement in South Africa, an issue which has created much moral consternation in recent years, presents another case in which American government regulation is either inoperable or inapplicable.

To sum up this discussion of the objections to the notion of corporate responsibility: these points do carry weight with respect to some affirmative modes of corporate social action,[62] but we find these objections unpersuasive in application to self-regulating activity. Whatever debate there may be over more expansive notions of corporate responsibility, a self-policing attempt to take into account the social consequences of business activity and at least attempt to avoid or correct social injury represents a basic obligation.[63]

SHAREHOLDERS AND CORPORATE RESPONSIBILITY

Even if the preceding conclusions about corporate responsibility are accepted, some critics would balk at assigning the shareholders any role in the process of corporate self-regulation. Three reasons are recited for such resistance: First, the shareholder, it is said, has no intrinsic relationship to corporate decision-making and control and therefore cannot really be said to participate in—to have responsibility for—social injury caused by corporate activity. As a result, any action undertaken by a shareholder to correct social injury does not serve the interests of his own self-regulation, but amounts to regulating others (in this case, management) and meddling in affairs that are not appropriate for shareholders. Second, shareholder participation in social matters is characteristically unfair in several different ways. Finally, shareholders are incompetent to deal with these issues. In short, shareholder participation is variously disparaged as illegitimate, unfair, and incompetent.

Legitimacy

The principal cause of uncertainty about the role of the shareholder is the now-familiar separation between corporate ownership and corporate control, first heralded in 1932 by Adolf Berle and Gardiner Means:

> A large body of security holders has been created who exercise virtually no control over the wealth which they or their predecessors in interest have contributed to the enterprise. In the case of management control, the ownership interest held by the controlling group amounts to but a very small fraction of the total ownership. Corporations where this separation has become an important factor may be classed as quasi-public in character in contradistinction to the private, or closely held, corporation in which no important separation of ownership and control has taken place.[64]

J. A. C. Hetherington has noted that "we have no consensus on what, if anything, ought to be done to remedy a situation generally considered anomalous."[65] Much of the scholarly writing since 1932 has denied the need for a remedy; it has been an attempt to redefine shareholding as something other than ownership. Edward Mason has written that "the equity owner is joining the bond holder as a functionless *rentier*,"[66] and others have noted that the vocabulary used by investors and financial advisors reflects more of Las Vegas than of John Locke on private property.[67] Hetherington has gone further, using the analog of "vendor and purchaser":

> The buyer of an equity security, whether he acquires it from the issuer or a prior holder, is a customer of the management. The product that he buys is the future profitability of the corporation, in which he expects to participate through distributions and market performance of the stock. In some respects the law has recognized this aspect of the shareholder's role. The Securities Act of 1933 and many of the state blue-sky laws are in spirit and function consumer-protection legislation.[68]

Furthermore, legal and administrative barriers impeding proxy fights by shareholders, the expense involved in waging such fights, and statutes defining the relative rights and duties of managers and stockholders (including, for example, the various statutory burdens imposed on shareholders who wish to bring derivative suits against management) have all served to solidify management's power and freedom in relation to the shareholder.[69]

It appears, therefore, that although there may be little consensus about what ought to be done to remedy the anomaly, there is considerable consensus on what ought not to be done: namely, to establish effective shareholder control.[70] So Abram Chayes writes:

> Shareholder democracy, so-called, is misconceived because the shareholders are not the governed of the corporation whose consent must be sought. If they are, it is only in the most limited sense. Their interests are protected if financial information is made available, fraud and overreaching are prevented, and a market is maintained in which their shares may be sold. A priori, there is no reason for them to have any voice, direct or representational, in the catalog of corporate decisions . . . on prices, wages, and investment. They are no more affected than nonshareholding neighbors by these decisions. In fine, they deserve the voiceless position in which the modern development left them.[71]

In the face of the shareholder's relative impotence in corporate government, what are the grounds for maintaining that the shareholder has and should exercise responsibility for the social consequences of corporate conduct?

We grant that the shareholder is not the cause of social injury in the same sense that the manager who fashions corporate policy is the cause of injury resulting from that policy. We are nevertheless convinced that owning shares in a corporation does thrust upon the owner a responsibility for the social effects of corporate policy that he would not otherwise have. In other words, the conditions of the Kew Gardens Principle (p. 22)—which create responsibility for social injury even if it is not clearly self-caused—apply to the position of the shareholder in relation to corporate-caused injury. *Need* is assumed from the presence of social injury. *Proximity, capability* and *last resort* require some discussion.

Proximity. What is it about being a legal "owner" that ties the shareholder into corporate policy and its social consequences? In the first place, there is the matter of notice. The Securities Exchange Act of 1934 and the rules of the exchanges require that the managements of listed companies provide a considerable amount of information to the shareholder about corporate affairs. Although this information does not necessarily include data relating to questions of social impact, it may alert shareholders to these issues. The shareholder is then free, upon a showing of reasonable cause, to inspect corporate records pertaining to these matters[72] and also to propose by-laws requiring that information relating to social injury be delivered to shareholders.

Access to information about corporate policy is, then, available or potentially available to shareholders in a way that it is not available to others who might be interested in the corporation's activities. As we have seen, notice—actual or "constructive"—of social injury is at least one of the conditions for the existence of an obligation to help to correct social harm.

The question of constructive notice raises the issue of *relationship*—and the general expectation that persons with a particular relationship to an institution ought to inform themselves about it. Whatever legal restrictions have been placed on the shareholder vis-à-vis management, and whether or not the shareholder has proprietary concern for the company, the law still defines the shareholder as an owner. As long as this doctrine is respected in any form—as long as the formal relationship is one of ownership—it would seem that some expectations must arise about the shareholder's responsibility for inquiring into the activities of the corporation. The law, after all, recognizes no one else as the possesser of ownership responsibilities (even though these responsibilities do not ordinarily entail legal liability for corporate acts). And although Bayless Manning believes that "the reform efforts of the corporate democrats . . . appear fundamentally mis-placed, misdirected and romantic," William Cary notes that Man-ning "cannot find a satisfactory alternative."[73]

It is possible that, on some questions, one can expect more "ownership" concern from certain groups of shareholders than from others. Perhaps a nonprofit institution, chartered to serve the public good and receiving certain benefits as such, should take more pains than other shareholders to examine the social impacts of the corporations in which it owns stock.

Capability. Much of the debate about shareholder power has focused on the question of whether shareholders either have or should have *control* over corporate policies. Hetherington, for example, maintains that "[e]fforts to place control in the hands of shareholders have totally misconceived the situation."[74] To have control over a decision is one thing; but to *influence* a decision is quite another. Hetherington notices this distinction but relegates it to a footnote on attempts to restore shareholder power:

It does not follow that such shareholder activities are entirely futile, however. The extent to which management proposals are modified, or even withheld, because of token stockholder oppo-sition and the possibility of adverse publicity cannot be accu-rately estimated, but it may be considerable. Thus, shareholder proposals and activism may have a "healthy indirect impact" on corporate management.[75]

It seems likely that the only managers who would be imper-vious to such impact are those who make decisions in total iso-lation for reasons dictated chiefly by whim or dogma. Most mana-gers probably do not act in this way. The increased power resting in their hands has created what Richard Eells has called a "con-stitutional crisis" in legitimacy and accountability.[76] Managers have tended to handle this crisis by serving as a kind of internal judicial system, balancing the various claims made on them by their constituencies—stockholders, consumers, suppliers, labor, and the general public. As part of this process, management depends upon the flow of communication from a multitude of sources, particularly including these constituencies.[77] This communication calls attention to problems, suggests solutions and alternatives, and in general prevents stagnation. Any addition (or reduction) of such information and opinion in some way influences the managers' decisions. As one of the several constituencies—and apart from legal "ownership" rights—the stockholders have power under this system.

But beyond the general influence of the various constituencies, the shareholder can also vote his stock, propose resolutions, hold forth at annual meetings, demand access to corporate information and bring derivative and individual shareholder law suits. He and his peers have the power to end injurious policies in a way that the other constituencies do not. And although shareholder power is fractional—only in rare circumstances would shareholder power be controlling—so also is almost all power, unless it is that of a despot. Most action we take in the public realm is part of the action of a larger group and becomes effective for this reason. To argue that fractional power should not be exercised would radically undermine the principle of democratic voting, wherein the majority has power because of the simultaneous exercise of fractional power by many individuals and the minority voice is understood to be significant simply because it has been heard. In the case of shareholder influence, this voting power must be understood not only in terms of concerted action with other shareholders, but also as a reinforcement of other sources and forms of influence on management, such as debate within the board room, government persuasion, general public concern, and the activities of the mass media.

At this juncture, a pragmatic objection may be raised. We have drawn an analogy between the fractional power of the voter in a democracy and the fractional power of the shareholder. The analogy may not be perfect, however: the voter in a political system, unless he is a member of a very small or minority party, has some reasonable expectation that his party or candidate may win. If the corporate shareholder has, in fact, no equivalent expectation of tangible effect, then all talk about shareholder power to influence management is true in theory alone.

On this question of actual impact, we present a brief discussion of the devices available to stockholders for influencing corporate policy and a look at the recent employment of these devices. We list here a dozen devices available for shareholder response to corporate activity considered socially harmful, in a roughly ascending order of aggressiveness:

1. Declining to invest
2. Divestment
3. Posing questions to management or urging management to change its policies in certain respects
4. Withholding proxies from management or abstaining on certain socially related resolutions proposed by other shareholders
5. Voting in opposition to management on such resolutions
6. Voting to unseat management in favor of opposition slates proposed by other stockholders
7. Undertaking to propose the resolutions or slates referred to in items 5 and 6 on the shareholder's own initiative
8. Soliciting proxies from other shareholders in order to carry out item 7
9. Joining other shareholders who are bringing litigation (derivative or individual) to enjoin certain corporate conduct
10. Bringing the litigation referred to in item 9 on the shareholder's own initiative
11. Taking any of the actions listed above pursuant to an agreement for concerted action with other shareholders
12. Making public announcements in connection with any of the actions listed above[78]

The first response (declining to invest) does not represent an attempt to influence management. Some shareholders may choose to stay out of certain industries or corporations whose products or policies they find objectionable: churches have long abstained from tobacco and liquor stocks. But such abstention will not correct or avert anything; at most, the shareholder can claim that he is not "linked" to a practice or industry that is morally repugnant to him.

We have already expressed our dissatisfaction with attempts to cleanse a portfolio through the sale of morally or socially objectionable holdings.[79] Such efforts, we maintained, tend to involve one in illusions about moral purity. But it has been suggested by some that divestment can be effective, either through the symbolic effect it will have on management (if the sale is accompanied, for example, by a public statement) or through the depression of market prices when a large number of shares are dumped at one time. With regard to the former contention, we agree that some symbolic effect may accompany the sale of stock. For reasons discussed more fully in chapter 3, we advocate such action when other attempts to correct or avert a serious wrong have failed. (We note here that for the small individual shareholder who has no resources for initiating stockholder action, divestment with protest to management may be the only recourse.) Concerning the latter contention—that the sale of shares will depress market prices—it seems unlikely that any imaginable sale could be large enough to have such an effect. Few institutions hold a sufficient percentage of outstanding stock in a single corporation to wield such power.[80] Furthermore, any price reduction that might take place would probably be very temporary—since it would not be based on unfavorable business prospects—and would therefore permit investors who were not morally motivated to realize an easy windfall profit.

The other responses on the above list invoke stockholder powers, some exercised in cooperation with others, some with accompanying publicity. Whether a shareholder chooses to engage in the more aggressive and perhaps more expensive devices will depend on the nature of the shareholder, the gravity of the issue involved, and the relative success of other means of redress. (In chapter 3 and in the Guidelines, we indicate how a university might choose among the various options.) All of these modes of exercising shareholder prerogatives share one distinct advantage over divestment or initial refusal to invest: they permit the iso-lation and correction of specific corporate activities or policies rather than the blanket indictment implied in the first two modes of response.

A recent court decision is likely to increase shareholder opportunities to exercise voting rights on social injury questions. In July 1970, the United States Court of Appeals for the District of Columbia Circuit instructed the Securities and Exchange Commission to reconsider its decision to support Dow Chemical's refusal to include in its annual proxy statement a shareholder proposal suggesting a charter amendment to prohibit manufacture of napalm.[81] The resolution had been proposed by the Medical Committee for Human Rights but had been rejected by management on the grounds discussed in chapter 5 (p. 134). The SEC supported Dow's position pursuant to existing SEC regulations. The court decided that the SEC's action was reviewable (this decision is now on review in the Supreme Court), but before ruling on the matter referred it to the SEC for explanation of its position. The court indicated its outlook, however. It noted that Dow management's position, if allowed to stand, would successfully eliminate a shareholder voice on any social issue. The court wrote:

> We think that there is a clear and compelling distinction between management's legitimate need for freedom to apply its expertise in matters of day-to-day business judgment, and management's patently illegitimate claim of power to treat modern corporations with their vast resources as personal satrapies implementing personal political or moral predilections.[82]

The case is not over, but the court's preliminary statement of its views presages a greater degree of shareholder freedom to introduce proposals relating to corporate social policy.[83]

Several shareholder confrontations with corporate management in the past few years give some indication of the type of effect that may reasonably be expected to follow from the exercise of shareholder voting rights, together with the proposing of resolutions and the informal persuasion of management.

It is at least probable that the expression of shareholder views in the 1967 annual meeting of Eastman Kodak was an important factor in persuading that corporation to resume negotiations with a community group (FIGHT) which had been protesting Kodak's hiring and other employment practices.[84]

In 1970, a small but well-funded group of shareholders sought to obtain proxies in support of several resolutions concerning General Motors' social policies. Despite widespread coverage in the news media, it was evident to all concerned from the beginning that the resolutions would be defeated easily. The voting at the meeting more than vindicated these expectations. But in spite of abundant reason to be confident of victory, GM management showed its concern by dispatching highly placed representatives to the offices and board rooms of many educational, religious, and other eleemosynary stockholders, defending GM's record on issues of minority opportunity, pollution, and safety. The entire battle called public attention to a number of problems of social and environmental import and occasioned a great deal of discussion of stockholder duties and powers and corporate responsibility within boards of trustees of many institutions which held GM stock and had to decide how to vote at the annual meeting. Within GM, it is almost certain that several actions are directly attributable to this shareholder campaign: the election of Leon Sullivan, a black minister experienced in minority economic development, to the board of directors; the constitution of a board committee to oversee GM's public policy impacts; and the creation of a committee of eminent ecologists to monitor the effects of GM's operations on the environment.

Campaign GM waged another round with GM management in 1971. Two of the resolutions proposed by *Campaign GM*—one permitting nonmanagement nominees for the board of directors to be listed in the corporation's proxy materials, and one giving three constituent groups the power to nominate directors—gained only 1.4 per cent and 1.1 per cent of the total vote, respectively. But the third proposal, which would have required management disclosure of data concerning the hiring of minorities, pollution control, and auto safety, received 2.4 per cent of the vote. (There are some corporate officials who would contend that whenever a shareholder proposal gets more than 2 per cent of the vote at an annual meeting, management considers this a serious matter.) Another shareholder proposal at the 1971 GM meeting came from the Episcopal Church, asking that GM terminate its operations in South Africa. The proposal received 1.3 per cent of the vote.

Similar campaigns were waged by shareholders of the Gulf Oil and Honeywell companies in 1971. As in the GM case, these efforts failed to achieve the 3 per cent vote which, under SEC rules, would have prevented the managements from excluding the same proposals on the proxy statements for the next year. (The Gulf Angola Project received about 1¼ per cent of the vote on two of its proposals calling for disclosure on social issues and the constitution of a committee to study Gulf's involvement in Angola.[85])

A very recent shareholder movement in a mutual fund received much more support than the cases we have just discussed. A proposal made at the Fidelity Trend Fund annual meeting, demanding that the Fund review the pollution and civil rights records of companies being considered for investment, received more than 12 per cent of the shareholder vote in spite of management opposition. One of the leaders of the movement, associate dean Roy Schotland of the Georgetown University Law Center, had said before the vote that anything over 3 per cent support would be "a victory"; the *Wall Street Journal* wrote that the proposal received "surprising support."[86] Socially oriented shareholder proposals offered at the A.T.&T. and Potomac Electric Power meetings in 1971 received more than 4 per cent of the votes—over 7 per cent in one case.

On balance, we would not expect the exercise of shareholder rights to occasion sudden, drastic reforms. It can, however, significantly alter decisions by management and may in some cases prevent or limit social injury. As two Princeton economists have noted, "Although there is a tendency to exaggerate the effectiveness of this type of pressure, there is evidence that corporations cannot fail to heed the admonitions of even small minorities of shareholders."[87] In many situations, the raising of a thoughtful question by a shareholder at the right moment may have this effect even when unaccompanied by voting or other action. The full effectiveness of such action is in large part still unexplored, and there is every indication that opportunity for this exploration will increase in the near future as a result of increasing shareholder concern about corporate social policy.

Summing up the topic of shareholder capability, it is the power to act that gives the corporate shareholder a responsibility that, for example, the corporate bondholder or noteholder does not have. If this power to intervene is what thrusts obligation upon the holder of a voting security, it can logically make no difference that the power was received casually, that it was not the reason for purchasing the security, that it was a by-product (perhaps an undesirable one) of a total return decision made for reasons like those which motivate the bondholder or noteholder. Similarly, a corporation that produces industrial waste might prefer not to have an impact on the environment; certainly, power over the environment was not the reason it built its plants. Yet the wish cannot wipe out the fact, and the fact—of power—must be faced. So it is with the holders of voting stock.

The *capability* of the shareholder to effect corporate change therefore contributes to his culpability if he does not act. This conclusion however, does not arise from some notion of collective guilt. Collective guilt ignores individual efforts to reverse the collective decision; collective guilt indicts the controlling faction and the dissenter alike. Our view does not ignore the role of the individual; on the contrary, our notion of individual responsibility turns entirely on the individual's own action rather than on the majority outcome. Thus, where the individual shareholder fails to do what he or it reasonably can do to seek to bring about corrective action by the shareholders as a group, that individual shareholder contributes—however fractionally—to the continuation of the corporate wrong. The shareholder's own vote or voice may well have been ineffective, but to fail to use it at all—to fail to test it—amounts to participation in the injurious practice.[88] It follows that an action taken to avoid participating in a corporate wrong is, on the part of the actor, an aspect of self-regulation.

Last Resort. Turning to the final Kew Gardens criterion, the shareholder may be considered as the last resort in cases of corporate-caused social injury. Within the corporation, when all efforts (whether through persuasion or other means) to change an injurious policy have failed, the shareholder has the last opportunity to end or avert that injury, either by removing the directors or amending the corporate charter to prohibit the wrong. In a broader sense, if the directors do not end or correct an injury on their own, and if there is no governmental intervention (whether because of ineptitude or lack of jurisdiction), then the shareholder represents the last resort.

Of course, any one shareholder might hope and expect that his peers will act. A warning made earlier is pertinent here: in complex organizations, it is frequently difficult to know whether other help is coming. This fact makes it all the more imperative that a shareholder who has responsibility thrust upon him (by virtue of proximity and capability), not fail to act in the vague hope that someone else will help or that "things will work themselves out."

To sum up this discussion of legitimacy, shareholder responsibility for corporate social injury follows from the application of the Kew Gardens principle, and this responsibility provides the shareholder with a legitimate basis for action.[89]

As a postscript, for some observers the Kew Gardens analysis is not necessary to reach the conclusion that shareholders are legitimate participants in corporate social questions. David Bayne has written:

> Insofar as the shareholder has contributed an asset of value to the corporate venture, insofar as he has handed over his goods and property and money for use and increase, he has not only the clear right, but more to the point, perhaps, he has the stringent duty to exercise control over that asset for which he must keep care, guard, guide, and in general be held seriously responsible.
>
> . . . as much as one may surrender the immediate disposition of [his] goods, he can never shirk a supervisory and secondary

duty (not just a right) to make sure these goods are used justly, morally and beneficially.[90]

Fairness

The first of several questions relating to fairness concerns the quality of shareholder action. Are we advocating a mode of activity that will open the door to an endless stream of mindless or frivolous or harassing complaints, demands, and resolutions by shareholders moved more by narcissism than social concern?[91] Will the corporate enterprise be subjected to unreasonable and arbitrary demands by stockholders?

The existing regulatory system provides some safeguards against such an outcome. The SEC rules on shareholder proposals contain some antiharassment features. For example, SEC Rule 14a-8 excuses the management from printing in its materials any shareholder proposal which failed to attract a certain percentage of votes at the prior annual meeting. And, even as putatively refined by the *Medical Committee for Human Rights* case, the rule would also relieve the management from circulating proposals raising social questions not related to the corporation's business. The securities laws and regulations also bar false and misleading claims in shareholder campaigns. We do not advocate any activity which goes beyond these restraints. And for the institutional shareholder that observes the Guidelines we are proposing, there is another limiting principle: the Guidelines, in defining *social injury,* emphasize the frustration or violation of legal rules, thus attempting to locate cause for shareholder actions in external norms rather than in individual predilection.

Apart from possible shareholder mindlessness, the concern for fairness may have another focus: because so large a portion of outstanding common stock is held by institutional investors, the measures we are advocating for such investors will in some way distort the decision-making process within the corporate polity. In much the same way that corporate bigness is feared when business enters into the moral and social arena, so also big institutional shareholders may be feared when they take social positions within the corporate world. There is the danger that large institutions will impose their social and moral points of view on managers and on other shareholders.

If there is any threat from the power of large institutional shareholders, however, this power is already being deployed. Advocates of shareholder action in cases of social injury ask only that the institutional investors occasionally reverse the direction in which that power is now exercised, i.e., in support of management policies. There is no apparent reason why opposition to management on questions of corporate-caused social injury is any more domineering than acquiescence or active support. (And if the power of institutional investors is strong enough to control the outcome of corporate policy disputes, it underlines the extent to which such investors, by failing to oppose socially injurious practices, may be said to *cause* them—more so than we were willing to grant in the preceding pages.)

Moreover, statements about institutional power in the stock market must be received with caution. Institutions have slowly increased their proportion of total holdings of common stock, having held, for example, 28.4 per cent of total stock in 1960 and 33.4 per cent in 1970.[92] But individuals still hold two thirds of all outstanding shares. Because it is usually impossible to organize individual shareholders in large public corporations into a cohesive opposition bloc, the history of shareholder voting has been that these shareholders tend to acquiesce in existing policies by voting for management or failing to vote at all. In other words, this two-thirds can be counted on for support of management on most issues. Thus the institutions do not outweigh the strength of management in most large companies.[93] Indeed, fairness may well suggest that it is helpful for institutional investors to assert their shareholder rights sufficiently to serve as a countervailing challenge to the overwhelming power now held by the management in social as well as other matters.

Finally, we are proposing only that institutional investors act individually; we are not suggesting that they should all band together as a power bloc. Although many of them will agree on some issues that come before shareholders, it seems unreasonable to suppose that all institutional shareholders will think alike on all moral and social questions. The variety of institutional responses to *Campaign GM* in 1970 and 1971 illustrates this point: as noted in chapter 1, some institutional shareholders voted against *Campaign GM;* some did so but wrote a letter criticizing management's performance; some abstained; some voted for the *Campaign GM* proposals; and some voted *Yes* on one proposal and *No* on the other.

The problem of fairness also arises in another context, to which Friedman has addressed himself: "In most of these cases, what is in effect involved is some stockholders trying to get other stockholders (or customers or employees) to contribute against their will to 'social' causes favored by the activities. Insofar as they succeed, they are again imposing taxes and spending the proceeds."[94] Apart from Friedman's use of taxation language to characterize this process, the assertion that stockholders will be coerced into taking social action "against their will" may mean that a small number of shareholders will cause the management to ignore the wishes of the majority. In that event, however, the majority has its remedies at the next annual meeting. Or Friedman may mean that the majority, by approving socially oriented activities, coerces the minority. If so, the point must be that many or most stockholders invest with the intention of making profits only, and that to cause the corporation to deviate from this sole standard violates some implicit compact to which the shareholders adhered or on which they relied when they purchased shares.

This question of a compact, and of minority rights implicit therein, has not been explored in the legal literature. (See note 4 on p. 194.) But if there is such a compact, it must be inferred from shareholder understandings and expectations, the character of which is subject to change over time. The current attitudes of shareholders who wish to promote self-regulation of corporate conduct must be considered, along with earlier, possibly more commercial, attitudes as a part of the overall historical pattern of expectations. Both the new and old, the mercenary and the altruistic, must be averaged in when we try to explicate the rules of the game. Moreover, even if the expectations were static, it is hard to believe that they would wholly exclude concern about social injury. Finally, what would constitute evidence for such expectations or understandings? One could take polls, or conduct historical studies, but we suspect that the evidence on expectations would prove ambiguous. In any event, we believe there is now no adequate foundation for an assumption that it is unfair to a shareholder minority for the majority to direct a correction of social injury.

Indeed, this last aspect of the fairness question—the inquiry into shareholder expectations—suggests an additional basis for shareholder involvement in corporate social issues. Corporate managers often cite shareholder pressures as a reason for not undertaking the correction of social injury or for not embarking on programs of affirmative action; i.e., the managers represent that the understandings and expectations of the shareholders tolerate no departure from profit maximization. To the extent that the management thus purports to speak for and take action at the behest of the shareholders, those shareholders who do not share the attitudes attributed to them are entitled—some would say obliged—to correct the record by taking shareholder action reflecting their true position.

Competence

Although there may be no basis for the notion that unfairness will result from the attempt of shareholders (and especially institutional shareholders) to influence management on social and moral issues, it may still be argued that they are incompetent to act in this way. In announcing its decision to vote against the resolutions proposed by *Campaign GM* in May of 1970, the Harvard Corporation stated that "in our view, the Board of Directors and not the stockholders of a corporation constitute the proper body for the determination of difficult questions of allocation of resources."[95]

Why this should be the case is not at all clear. The wisdom required to decide questions of social policy and social injury is diffuse; no one profession or vocation is uniquely qualified to find solutions to the problems which beset the society. Management, without a doubt, is best equipped to handle the day-to-day business decisions of a corporation; but where those decisions have a wider social effect—and especially where they cause harm to others—the competence to assess that effect (and perhaps to decide to reverse it) is not a matter of special managerial expertise.

Doubts about competence sometimes flow from fears that information about corporate social policies and impacts is too difficult to obtain. Although the small individual shareholder may well encounter this problem, the institutional shareholder has a variety of sources available to it: reports of specialized government agencies and interest groups, congressional committees, corporate annual reports, information from brokerage and investment advisory firms, and independent research groups.[96] The pressure generated by special interest groups, shareholders, and possibly government agencies as well, will probably increase the volume of information disseminated to the shareholders by the corporations themselves.

Finally, the issue of competence is too frequently used as a paralyzing argument: it is too difficult to make the judgments required to resolve social issues in a very complex society. Many of the social questions facing us today are complicated, and in many cases certain social imperatives are apparently contradictory; for example, it is difficult to reconcile the demand for full employment with the demand for an improved environment or quality of life. But inaction in the face of difficulty is just as likely to compound the problems as it is to prevent them. And although it is not always possible to foresee the consequences of an attempt to resolve certain problems, it is only through the experience of trial and error that we are likely to find new ways of coping with them.

We conclude, then, that on the basis of the shareholder's unique relation to the corporation and his power to influence management and change corporate practice, the shareholder bears responsibility for harm resulting from corporate business practices; further, we conclude that shareholder activity consistent with this responsibility does not represent a major problem from the standpoint of fairness and competence.

But there is one final pragmatic objection which must be addressed: if one wants to minimize the amount of social injury done by the corporation, the last way to do it is to goad the shareholder into action, because most shareholders will wind up on the wrong side of every question. From this viewpoint, the attempt to involve shareholders in social and moral questions opens a Pandora's Box, permitting reactionary shareholders to win the day. Some corporate managers have suggested, for example, that managers on the whole are more public-spirited and socially conscious than shareholders as a whole, and that shareholders, if given a chance, would only limit what managers would like to do to fulfill their public responsibilities.[97]

We are puzzled about what would constitute proof on either side of this point. There are probably many corporate managers who are willing to go far beyond their stockholders' wishes in serving what appears to be the public interest. But against this must be weighed the history of many corporate managements who led their companies into price-fixing and other criminal activities for which shareholder approval would not likely have been forthcoming. And for every aggressively mercenary stockholder, there is likely to be another willing to own stock in a company that pollutes less or makes safer products, despite a sacrifice in return.

But even more important is that the Pandora's Box objection seems to rest on a strange principle: that the corporate system depends for its health on ignorance and silence rather than on healthy debate—that certain questions ought not to be asked for fear of getting inconvenient answers. While shareholders may prove, in the short run, to be less concerned for the public interest than some advocates of shareholder responsibility hope, in the long run society will benefit from more widespread participation in moral and social issues. Keeping people away from these issues only increases the atrophy of responsibility already pervasive in a highly organized society. The fabric of trust, so essential for a democratic nation, rests on the reciprocal expectation that persons and institutions will take responsibility for the social consequences—intended or unintended—of their acts.

3. The University as Responsible Investor

THE BASIC POLICY

The argument pertaining to the investing university which most directly follows from the preceding chapter—and which will henceforth be called the *Basic Policy*—can be stated as follows:

The "moral minimum" responsibility of the shareholder to take such action as he can to prevent or correct corporate social injury extends to the university when it is a corporate shareholder.

We have noted earlier that not all citizens can be charged with the same set of responsibilities. On the one hand, it is conceivable that there are persons or institutions that cannot be expected to act on the prima facie obligation to reduce or eliminate certain kinds of social injury, since their efforts to meet that level of responsibility either will be incompetent (and thus counterproductive) or will defeat socially important purposes which they, as individuals or organizations, are committed or organized to pursue. On the other hand, there are citizens whose responsibilities go well beyond the "moral minimum," since they are sufficiently powerful or sufficiently competent, or both, to be able to assume these more extensive obligations, and since in doing so they implement (or at least do not frustrate) their primary purposes.

Those who criticize the Basic Policy have argued that the university falls into one or the other of these two camps. Some contend that in the case of a university, compelling reasons can be given for not considering moral and social aspects of investment policy, either because the university is not competent to do so, or because doing so will prevent it from pursuing its primary mission of education.[1] By contrast, others argue that university responsibilities in the investment area extend well beyond the "moral minimum" precisely because of the university's purpose and competence in education.

Both points of view have some merit. The university is an anomalous institution. It has purposes and goals which make it an unusually fragile and vulnerable institution—a point which seems self-evident today. Moreover, the university may not be particularly well organized *as an institution* to render social and moral judgments and to act upon them. On the other hand, the purposes and goals for which the university *is* organized—the criticism and transmission of ideas and methods—do make it an institution within which individuals constantly make implicit and explicit judgments about normative issues with unusual care and precision and thus, presumably, competence.

Both of these perspectives deserve careful attention in order to test the Basic Policy. This chapter is structured to respond to each of them in turn by treating these questions:

Is it appropriate for a university to take moral and social issues into account by honoring the Basic Policy?

If so, what refinements and qualifications of the Basic Policy are required?

How are these refinements to be incorporated into a set of operating guidelines?

Do the Guidelines—drafted to meet fears about the Basic Policy—represent an excessively timid approach?

Can one assess the overall costs and benefits of adopting our proposed Guidelines?

Before proceeding, it is essential to describe the kinds of colleges and universities to which we refer, for not all institutions of higher learning subscribe to the same statement of nature and purpose.

As a result of the founding circumstances or later evolution, many American colleges and universities are organized to foster specifiable social and moral purposes through the educational process. Some, for example, were founded by religious organizations to educate in the light of a particular religious understanding or tradition; moral and social views are implicit or explicit in the incorporating charter, in the past positions taken by the institution, or in contemporary self-definitions offered by institutional officers (including the faculty).

Many of these institutions have, over the years, disavowed previously held social and moral commitments. Yale University is an institution of this sort. One may still read in Yale's charter (1745) that "... Yale College ... has trained up many Worthy Persons for the Service of God in the State as well as in the Church." It is clear from the context that the drafters of this statement considered the defining purpose of the institution to be the continuance of this "training up." In its modern history, however, Yale has come to concentrate most heavily upon two other statements of purpose in the preamble to the same charter:

1. The charter recites that Yale was earlier founded as an institution "wherein Youth might be instructed in the Arts and Sciences ...."
2. The preamble states that the petitioners for the charter had asked that "such other additional Powers and Privileges ... be granted as such be necessary for the Ordering and Managing of the Said School in the most advantageous and beneficial manner for the promoting of all good Literature in the present and Succeeding Generations."

These statements constitute almost exclusively the contemporary definition of Yale's mission, as set forth by President Kingman Brewster: "It is above all else a place to advance knowledge and to assist students to share in and help create that knowledge. By a tradition we share with all western universities worthy of the name, we are committed to pursuit of this goal by encouraging students and faculty alike to examine competing and conflicting views and to bring their full talents to bear in making objective and fearless choice among the alternatives of importance."[2]

The history of American education is, in part, the history of a struggle to allow the student and the scholar freedom of inquiry, when their search for knowledge has led to conclusions incompatible with the orthodoxies of the school's founders, administrators, or supporting constituencies. This history is superficially interpreted if viewed as the secularization of American education. It is better understood as the freeing of the academic enterprise from institutional orthodoxies of any sort.

As Yale's history illustrates, some schools accomplished this unfettering by permitting the disintegration of all institutional commitments to any values except the pursuit of knowledge for its own sake. Others accomplished it (or are accomplishing it) by discovering ways to maintain social value commitments while nevertheless encouraging both awareness and criticism of these values within the academic community.[3]

Universities which have taken the latter course will answer the questions raised by the notion of investment responsibility— Should we adopt a social investment policy? or On the basis of what criteria will it be guided?—in the light of their continuing social and moral value commitments. The relationship between freedom of inquiry and an institutional moral-social position on investments will raise no wholly new issues, will create no new tensions, for these schools. They struggle continually with these same basic issues, these same tensions, although the notion of social investment raises them in a different context. Indeed, even this context is not new for many of these schools, which have long allowed institutional positions to inform investment decisions at least to the point of refusing to purchase tobacco and liquor stocks.

We do not, however, concentrate here on universities with such social value commitments. Except where otherwise noted, the analysis offered in this chapter and the remainder of this book focuses *only* on the universities and colleges whose self-understanding has never included, or at least does not now include, any institutional value commitment except the pursuit of knowledge.[4] (This focus does not necessarily imply a belief that such a definition of a school's mission should or will remain unchanged. The issue of institutional commitment is now being debated in many schools, and if the results are substantial shifts in self-definition, the analysis and Guidelines offered here might well be altered.)

OBJECTIONS TO THE BASIC POLICY

Objections Related to Neutrality

Objection 1: Including moral and social considerations in investment policy would violate a university's institutional neutrality, an essential principle of all university decision-making.

At the outset we should point out that institutional neutrality is not necessarily what we have been discussing in our reference to universities without social value commitments. This point is illustrated by the fact that even those educational institutions that have explicit religious, moral, or social commitments are often concerned about institutional neutrality, and also by the fact that many critics are unwilling to concede that the absence of such commitments produces neutrality. In analyzing the neutrality objection, then, we are not simply rehearsing the discussion just completed.

That we must begin by stressing this threshold point is itself illuminating. Even though institutional neutrality is constantly invoked in discussions about the university—and in a variety of contexts—there is surprisingly little literature which clearly defines or interprets the concept.[5] Yet to determine what neutrality "means" for a university is rather difficult. Does *neutral* mean "not taking part in either side of a quarrel" or does it, alternatively, suggest taking a "middle position between extremes"?[6] Both are accepted definitions, but they point in quite different directions. For example, to some, being neutral means that an institution of higher education will not take stands, as an institution, on political or social questions. Often this prohibition is extended to the personal statements of a university's officers. But others do not think that neutrality has this meaning and hence do not oppose position-taking so long as it does not become controversial—that is, so long as it does not incur the wrath of those at either end of the spectrum of opinion on a given issue. Or, again, some have thought that neutrality means that instructors should not take sides in classroom debate, while others believe that a professor's classroom is his castle as long as his opinions are moderate. Some have averred that neutrality means that academic disciplines can and should start from a position independent of any cultural presuppositions, while others have argued that this view is naive and instead see academic study as seeking accommodation between extremes in debate over rival value claims. For still others, all of the preceding is beside the point since, for them, neutrality is closely linked with reason or rationality (whether it leads to moderate or extreme conclusions) but is always at odds with passion, desire, or subjective judgment.

Efforts to discover the quintessential meaning of *neutral* will lead to interminable debate and will yield little in the understanding of institutional neutrality.[7] It does not necessarily follow from this, however, that the concept is specious or does not have work to do. If we shift our focus from what institutional neutrality "means" to what its *function* is, we will be in a better position to determine whether or not an objection based on neutrality vitiates the Basic Policy.

Turning to function, we find that what all of these various and even contradictory appeals to neutrality appear to have in common is their effort to characterize the stance of a university which best preserves the conditions and atmosphere required for fostering academic work—particularly including the conditions for the maintenance of academic freedom, which is, in turn, a concept describing the right of scholars to pursue knowledge freely.[8] An environment which provides these ingredients we shall refer to as the *Academic Context.*[9] Where a university is able to foster an Academic Context, it has fulfilled the primary mission it has set for itself. It is required to do no more—and no less—than this.

Accordingly, perhaps one should say that a university is a place where the Academic Context is maintained, rather than that a university must maintain "institutional neutrality." And yet, in the tumult of the past several years, there has been more rather than less preoccupation with neutrality. In the process, this concept, whose ambiguities we noted earlier, has been reified. Some have asserted, without explanation, that neutrality is a good in itself, rather than a means to an end, an instrumentality for fostering a particular kind of environment. So conceived and applied, institutional neutrality either says too much or too little about what is required to protect the Academic Context, and it becomes dysfunctional. Three examples clarify this point. Two illustrate cases where uncritical application of the concept actually undermines the ability of the university to protect the Academic Context. The third case—the one which involves the subject of this report—demonstrates how applying institutional neutrality to all university activities, indiscriminately and without regard for its function, yields results other than the protection of the Academic Context.

First, as we have seen, the inference is sometimes drawn that neutrality requires teachers and students to be neutral in expressing their views in—and sometimes out of—the classroom. In fact, this notion *violates* a basic tenet of academic freedom. Freedom to express views on controversial matters is a dominant theme of the classic document in the field, the AAUP's *Academic Freedom and Tenure—Statement of Principles,* 1940.[10] (Although it originally related to faculty members, the academic freedom doctrine has been applied to students in subsequent AAUP pronouncements and court decisions.) Furthermore, an uncritical application of some definitions of neutrality might be interpreted wholly to preclude certain academic programs—indeed entire university departments or schools—on the ground that they espouse views which must be considered normative. This is especially true of professional schools that have a commitment to certain premises —for example, the value of healing through human intervention or the value of the rule of law. And a university divinity school is not neutral if neutrality means taking a middle course on religious matters; the school cannot train for the ministry in a particular religious tradition without accepting the strong religious commitments of that tradition.

Second, even the university as an entity cannot always remain neutral in the senses we have discussed. It does not and should not shun an adversary role in the face of external threats to the Academic Context. Witness, for example, the willingness of most schools to enter, directly and institutionally, into the legislative fray involving proposals to decrease or increase the resources needed to support academic life or the rights embraced by academic freedom.

Third, the neutrality issues raised by the social investment problem are quite different. In the process of creating and sustaining the Academic Context, a university does many things: it consumes goods and services; owns land; sometimes sells things; and *invests*. These activities are substantially different in character from the educational ones. In his article "What Business is a University In?" Irving Kristol emphasizes precisely this distinction in functions: "No university is merely a 'community of scholars.' In order for such a community to exist and survive, it needs to be buttressed by an organizational component, by an administration which manages money and real estate and employees and relations with the world outside."[11]

What would it mean to be neutral about administrative activities such as these? However difficult it may be to apply any meaning of neutrality to any aspect of university activity, it is particularly difficult to apply the concept to these supporting tasks. To carry out these functions, the university cannot avoid participation in the prevailing economic system. And in so doing, it usually reflects the values of that system. For example, it remunerates its employees on the basis of the market value of their services rather than on the basis of "each according to his need." On the other hand, the university sometimes departs sharply from the values of the prevailing system—when, for example, it charges its students a flat fee for medical services and then provides each student with services "according to his need." Even under more conventional tests of neutrality, we find that the administrative and economic activities of universities have not typically been accorded neutral treatment. For example, most universities became (or claimed to be) equal opportunity employers before they were required to do so by law.[12]

This area of administrative-economic activity points up, in acute form, that *institutional neutrality* is not a phrase which is helpful in describing the modus operandi of university activity.

Instead, *institutional neutrality* has served as the shorthand term to remind the university, at every turn, that measures must be taken to protect the Academic Context if the nature of the university is not to be subverted. That is the primary function of the expression.[13]

The only possible justification for treating neutrality as an operating principle, which purports to describe all activities of an educational institution, is tactical: by pointing to neutrality, the university might be able to persuade its participants and the society at large that the university's highest priority is its commitment to the academic enterprise—teaching and scholarly work—and the success of this argument might help the university to protect the Academic Context against external aggression. Later in this chapter we address the question whether, in the investment context, it is in fact necessary to flaunt neutrality for such public relations purposes. At this point, we emphasize that a university has been deceived by an ambiguous phrase if it does not recognize these difficulties when it makes unqualified appeals to institutional neutrality.

We conclude that the neutrality concept cannot serve as a reliable basis for a principled objection to the Basic Policy. But the neutrality discussion does (albeit indirectly) raise a rather different but important question: would the investment policy suggested by the Basic Policy damage the Academic Context? It is to that question—an essentially pragmatic inquiry—that we turn when considering the next two objections. The first of these contends that such an investment policy would deleteriously affect the *internal* conditions requisite to the maintenance of the Academic Context. The second objection requires us to consider whether such a policy would occasion actions (reprisals) by persons and/or groups *external* to the university, adversely affecting the Academic Context.

Objection 2: Including moral and social considerations in investment policy would so affect the character of a university's internal activity as to damage the Academic Context.

Those who raise this objection are concerned for the preservation of a university's raison d'être. They fear that if the university "takes political or social positions," through its investment programs or otherwise, this action will politicize or economically hobble the university—and thus harm the Academic Context. They fear, for example, that the introduction of social investment concepts will result in the development of ideological orthodoxies affecting university decisions on such matters as faculty hiring and student admission, or will occasion endless faculty debate of a divisive and distracting nature, or will result in the diversion of university resources (already in short supply) from academic programs.

These worries are analogous to those that have been voiced in opposition to the passage of "political" faculty resolutions. For example, 152 members of the Harvard Faculty of Arts and Sciences explained their objection to a Vietnam War resolution in these words:

1. The Faculty claims the right to function as a center of learning without political objectives. While no such center can be wholly objective or neutral, it must strive, however imperfectly, toward that end. Society will not long allow us the freedom if it appears that, as an institution, we have joined the political fray.
2. If debates on political matters, however important, become customary in the Faculty, then politics will enter into the evaluation of candidates for appointment to the Faculty.
3. By joining the Faculty, all members signify their willingness to be bound by majority decisions with respect to those matters about which the Faculty is authorized and competent to act. But few if any members joined with the understanding that they were to accept the right or competence of any part of the Faculty to speak for them on matters of conscience and politics.
4. Although those who advance a particular political cause may disavow any intention of setting a precedent, the precedent is nonetheless set. Since we will no longer be able to exclude political matters from the docket by appeal to rule and

precedent, we will be obligated to discuss each and to act on each on its merits. The proper concerns of the Faculty cannot long survive continued and inevitably impassioned political debate.[14]

If we are to give coherent consideration to the objection, we must first understand what the ingredients of the Academic Context are. Although this understanding is difficult to achieve, the available literature[15] —as well as recent debates over the taking of political positions by universities and faculties—points toward agreement that an Academic Context can be characterized as follows:

It is a place where all ideas and theories may be examined, criticized, and expounded, free from external or internal pressures. This requires that decisions concerning participation or advancement in the academy should not be made on the basis of particular social, political, or other views held by a faculty member or a student; actions by the institution should help maintain a climate which fosters this approach; where diversity of views (or potential diversity of views) exists, care must be taken that the institution's decisions do not suggest—or appear to suggest—that members of the academic community share a single view;[16] the scope and emphasis of academic activities should be shaped by members of the academic community (primarily faculty and students); and that community, in turn, should ensure that the academic process is open to all alternatives relating to the methodology and content of learning and research.[17]

An Academic Context is not only one in which orthodoxies are not permitted to *inhibit* work and exploration; it is also one in which the ethos or climate is *conducive* to academic pursuits. While knowledge may be acquired in a variety of atmospheres, an Academic Context is one in which the climate does not·unreasonably distract those engaged in disciplines that flourish best through sustained and orderly study; and it is one in which sufficient resources (remuneration, research facilities, etc.) are available to facilitate diverse activities of those who teach and learn.[18]

Need the Basic Policy undermine such a context? One can answer this question only by examining the investment criteria and procedures that are calculated to prevent such a result. Two underlying strategies have informed the development of such criteria and procedures: our Guidelines are devised to maintain *distance* between the Academic Context and the execution of the university's investment responsibilities; additionally, they are structured to assure *minimal distraction* from academic pursuits.

Distance. A recurring theme in the outline of the Academic Context we have just set forth is the notion that it is threatened by acts which tend toward the establishment of orthodoxies within the academic community. Thus, activities which imply that a university has a political or social position are feared because of the tendency for that position to spill over into the academic process and inhibit the free expression of views; one may also fear any action which causes the academic community to be wrongly perceived as the locus of decision-making on social or political issues—a misperception that might lead to the assumption that all members of the academic community are of a single mind on moral and social questions. The strategy of keeping as much distance as possible between the academic enterprise and investment decisions is intended to minimize both of these threats.

In fact, the maintenance of this separation is consistent with the central premise of the Basic Policy—that a university has social investment responsibilities because it is an institutional investor, not because it is a university. Investing, like many other administrative activities carried out by a university, is a function largely independent of the academic process; it is one in which the university is involved not as a result of what is being taught, learned, and investigated, but as a result of the necessity to support academic activities in a variety of ways. This distinction has important consequences for our analysis. If the locus of decision-making on social investment decisions were largely separated from the academic enterprise, and if the procedures and decision-making criteria emphasized and made clear this distinction, many fears concerning the politicization of the university would be reduced. This outcome could be achieved by adopting the Basic Policy but specifying the following conditions: those outside the academic community would have final decision-making authority; when members of the academic community were officially involved in any aspect of the deliberations, they would be present in administrative rather than academic capacities; and decisions by the university would be made in accordance with criteria generated primarily outside of the academic community.

Minimal Distraction. Even given the distance strategy, it is possible that either too much social investment activity, or certain types of it, would divert attention, energies, or resources from the academic enterprise. Hence, the necessity of a strategy specifically designed to prevent social investment activity from causing inordinate distraction. This approach, like the preceding one, is compatible with the primary thrust of the Basic Policy. That policy focuses on the minimal obligation of a citizen to regulate his socially injurious impacts or those of the institutions he inhabits; it does not propel its adherents into the uncharted waters of moral and social advocacy, where interminable debate (if not hopeless confusion) might well swamp the Academic Context.

A minimal-distraction strategy that seeks to avoid unnecessary involvement in moral and social controversy should incorporate the notion that the criteria employed in a university investment policy are to be generated primarily outside the academic community. Additionally, it should be made clear the advisory participation in decision-making should not be excessively time-consuming for members of the academic community; and the decisions should not often, if ever, require plenary participation of the academic community. That this Basic Policy is concerned with correcting deleterious impacts of the university's corporate involvements—in a form of self-regulation—and not with moral social engineering, should be underscored by a provision minimizing the university's role as an initiator of social investment activities. Finally, the scope of the university's involvement should not result in fiscal distraction—a diversion of the university's resources which financially impairs the Academic Context.

Incorporating these two strategies—distance and minimal distraction—into the implementation of the Basic Policy should rebut any assumption that a university's effort to meet its ethical minimum obligations will necessarily subvert the Academic Context. In other words, if these principles are honored, the Basic Policy ought not be inconsistent with maintenance of the Academic Context.

It is conceivable (but probably unlikely) that, despite these strategies, the actual implementation of the Basic Policy might lead to one or more of the feared impairments of the Academic Context. To deal with this contingency, a social investment program should include provisions which permit the university to refrain from acting in a particular controversy where harm to the Academic Context can be anticipated.

The safeguards mentioned above may be summed up in the following investment principles, where a university is to include moral and social considerations in its investment policy:

The locus of decision-making should be separated from the academic enterprise.

Criteria should be generated primarily by sources outside the academic community.

Criteria should be readily applicable to diverse and complex issues.

Decisions should be based on criteria generally acceptable to most of those within the academic community.

Plenary involvement of the entire university community in social investment decisions should be minimized or excluded.

Social investment decision-making should not become so time-consuming for the academic community that the educational process is impaired.

Except in unusual circumstances, the university should involve itself in social investment questions only if the issue is thrust upon it by other stockholders.

Social investment decisions should not impair the fiscal ability of the university to perform its educational functions.

Provisions should be made for a university to adjust its social investment practices in case of serious adverse consequences.

Objection 3: The public-at-large and the constituencies that support the university will perceive even a limited program built on the Basic Policy to be inappropriate and will retaliate against its implementation in such a way as to damage the Academic Context.

In the discussion of institutional neutrality, we noted the possible usefulness of this indeterminate concept for suggesting to those not within the university that it is willing to make the following compact with other persons and institutions: "We will stay out of your business, if you will stay out of ours." In other words, despite the illusory or indefinable quality of *neutrality,* it is widely perceived to have substance, and those who fear that external invasions will damage the Academic Context are leary of any university action which might alter this misunderstanding.

Robert Paul Wolff, a Columbia professor with strong anti-establishment credentials, has argued that the university should continue to use the neutrality concept for precisely this reason.[19] He establishes that neutrality is a "myth" in many respects. He contends nevertheless that the appearance of neutrality must be maintained so that the university may have some argument with which to deter outside forces (and perhaps alumni as well) from punishing radical and otherwise unorthodox faculty members and students. Although not exposing the myth, former Cornell University President James Perkins has asked: "If the universities begin to play the game of economic sanctions to influence corporate policy, are they prepared for similar strategy on the part of corporations towards the universities? Should we abandon the idea that has taken several centuries to secure, namely, that those who give financial support to the university should not try to use that support as a lever for influencing university policy? In a contest of economic coercion, does anyone really think the university would win?"[20]

There are three ways in which a university may attempt to meet this objection and yet deal with social injury aspects of its investments. First, the university should have a clear set of criteria and procedures—and a rationale for them—which it can use to explain to the various university constituencies that its participation in shareholder self-regulation of corporate social injury is not an economic sanction or economic coercion (to use Perkins' language), and that the social investment policies do not violate the university's purpose and function. Among other things, the procedures should make it clear that it is the administrative rather than the academic sector of the university which is taking action on social injury questions. Second, if the criteria for social and moral investment action look largely to external public policy norms, the university will be able to point out that it is not itself sitting in judgment but that—in administering its inevitable non-neutral economic activities—it is giving effect to the norms established by the society-at-large. (In our proposed Guidelines, the focus upon legal norms in establishing social investment criteria is, in part, an effort to find sources of authority external to the university.[21]) Finally, if these measures fail, any guidelines for social investment activities must offer a way of temporarily cutting back on these activities, should it appear that the apparent decline in neutrality is bringing on dangerous retaliation.[22]

If all three of these avenues are pursued seriously, we believe that this reprisal objection is vitiated. Again, we sum up the investment principles which emerge from this discussion (some of which overlap with principles set forth earlier) by concluding that if a university is to include moral and social considerations in its investment policy—

The locus of decision-making should be separated from the academic enterprise.

Social investment policies should be adopted only if a university is able to devise a process which will yield reasonably skillful and competent decisions.

Criteria should be generated primarily by sources outside the academic community.

Except in unusual circumstances, the university should involve itself in social investment questions only if the issue is thrust upon it by other stockholders.

Provisions should be made for the university to adjust its social investment practices in case of serious adverse consequences.

Objections Related to the Division of Labor Question

We now turn to several variations on what is often called the division of labor theme: that any one institution has limited capacities and should therefore devote its energies and resources to work that it can most competently perform, unless there are compelling reasons why it should assume other responsibilities. We shall examine each of the objections to the Basic Policy which the division of labor issue raises.

Objection 1: Through its educational function, the university serves to reinforce the values of a society and provide it with skilled leaders. In so doing it completely fulfills its citizenship obligations as an institution and need not concern itself with investment responsibility.

This premise concerning the university's role is widely held. The university's performance of the leadership-training function often appears to motivate alumni and governmental support. The failure to meet alumni expectations with respect to value-reinforcement is a source of recent dissatisfaction with some universities and may contribute to the present financial plight of higher education.

The dispositive response to this objection is not that a university has moral minimum investment responsibilities in spite of its training function, although such a case could undoubtedly be made. Instead, the basic flaw in this objection is confusion over the nature of a university. A university does often carry on leadership-training and does sometimes reinforce societal assumptions and traditions by teaching from materials which carry or explain or espouse those assumptions and traditions. But it is inconsistent with the nature and purpose of the university to describe either of these processes as a responsibility or task assignment, the fulfillment of which preempts other duties.

The universities' mission, as they have defined it, is to provide a place where the available values of a society are not only described but questioned. This activity may result in reinforcement of these values; but then again, it may not. As for leadership training, society may well find that students are best educated for leadership in those places where no value is left unquestioned; but then again, it may not. For the university, neither value-reinforcement nor leadership-training can be the dominant concern. Although others may see these as a university's primary functions, from the university's standpoint these are subordinate—or even latent—functions. Kingman Brewster seems to have been making this point when, in his address at the 1970 Carleton College commencement, he urged that alumni increase their unrestricted gifts to universities: ". . . unrestricted support presupposes that the alumnus believes in the place because of its intrinsic importance, not because it will solve his problems. . . ."

Hence, a university which argues that it is doing its total societal job—and should be burdened with no other responsibilities—when it fulfills its "function" of preparing students for leadership or reinforcing dominant values, has either lost sight of its own nature, or, in contemporary terms, is guilty of a truth-in-packaging or a truth-in-advertising violation. Institutions of higher education simply cannot guarantee that in their pursuit of knowledge they will necessarily produce precisely what the wider society wants. Their first job, as they themselves have described it, is to provide the Academic Context for learning and research.

Objection 2: The university's sponsorship of free inquiry serves an indispensable function in our society, and hence the university should concern itself solely with performance of that function.

The premise here is worthy. It certainly can be argued that a free society is radically dependent upon the existence of the free university—one place where men may reflect on the society's options in a manner precluded elsewhere.[23] It is not clear, however, why this premise compels the conclusion that a university should exclude social considerations from the discharge of its supportive and administrative tasks. In other words, this version of the division of labor view is no more helpful than the neutrality concept in guiding the university's conduct of its necessary economic activities (one of which is investing). It does provide, however, an added incentive for insisting that any social investment guidelines be written so as to protect the requisite Academic Context.

Objection 3: The university is not competent (or is especially incompetent) to make decisions on moral and social issues arising from ownership of corporate shares.

Irving Kristol is one of several persons in the academic community who has argued that universities are not competent to make decisions on moral and social matters because they are not only poorly organized to make collective decisions, but also have proven to be very bad at it.[24] The university, Kristol states, does not possess a "collective intelligence," and a community of scholars is simply not a political community. Kristol contends that only a community organized to render political judgments can do so effectively. Whether or not Kristol is correct on the structural point, the major burden of his argument is that scholars lack competence for this purpose. In this connection, he assumes that the decision-making body for the issues under discussion would be the faculty (as it has been until recently at Princeton, for example). His "scholarly incompetence" argument is largely irrelevant if the decisions are not made by the community of scholars itself.

We note, however, that one reason advanced by Kristol for his allegation of incompetence is that individual scholars are poor at making social and moral judgments requiring practical sagacity:

... social problems usually reflect conflicts of values—between different sections of the populations, of course, but also *within* the hearts and minds of the majority of individuals who compose the entire community.

The reason politics is such a difficult art is less that people are insufficiently enlightened and more that it is in the nature of human beings to want incompatible things at the same time. . . .

It is because our social problems are of this nature that the prime political virtue is, not theoretical rectitude, but practical sagacity (what the ancients used to call "prudence"). This is not an academic virtue; indeed, where it exists it can be an academic weakness. We want our social theorists to be bold and keen and unconstrained in the use they make of their imaginative and analytical powers. And it is precisely because we want this that we must look askance at the proposition that academic men ought, as a species, to get involved in the management of our society.[25]

Kristol's argument is, perhaps, on target with regard to some academic persons. Nevertheless, we believe that many other faculty members are competent decision-makers, partly because they bring to the task the experience of having thought through the implications of various social policy decisions.[26]

Kingman Brewster and other university administrators seem to be making a more general but related "competence" point: the university as an entity is not equipped to make social decisions. Brewster has said: "We are, in short, best prepared to be our brother's thinker. We have no special competence to be our brother's legislator or banker or diplomat or manager."[27] In the spring of 1970, another university administrator argued similarly, with reference to the *Campaign GM* proxy controversy, that his board of trustees did not possess the qualifications to make highly sophisticated decisions concerning the responsibilities of corporate management in pollution control and related matters.

The university will not, of course, have as much detailed technical knowledge about a company's problems as the company's own management. Yet the dilemmas of corporate responsibility are not exclusively—or, in many cases, largely—technical. The issue of how to implement a particular policy determination may have to be left to the management's experts, but the policy decision itself typically involves a wide range of economic, scientific, and social perspectives that cut across professional and occupational lines. Even if we could identify the kinds of persons especially competent to make these decisions, our society is not organized to ensure that these men and women would acquire the power to exercise their competence.

To the extent, however, that certain professional, scientific, and analytical skills are helpful in resolving these responsibility questions, they exist among members of the university community. In other words, resources are available to the university which should make it at least as competent in exercising its shareholder responsibilities as any other investing institution or group.

This last point suggests that if social and moral considerations are to play any part in a university's investment activities, efforts should be made to include, at some level of the decision-making process, members of the university community who have individual skills with respect to the issues involved. At this point, however, we encounter a potential conflict between the notion, mentioned earlier, that the faculty and student bodies engaged in the academic enterprise should not be responsible for making social or moral decisions, and the desirability of drawing on the competence of individual faculty or student members. Our suggested Guidelines attempt to resolve this conflict through the establishment of two levels of decision-making—an advisory level incorporating faculty and student members and a final decisional level involving only the trustees.

Objection 4: It is inefficient for a university to use its limited resources to deal with corporate responsibility questions.

The Committee on the University's Role in Political and Social Action (the Kalven committee) at the University of Chicago has raised the general problem as follows: "Our basic conviction is that a great university can perform greatly for the betterment of society. It should not, therefore, permit itself to be diverted from its mission into playing the role of a second-rate political force or influence."[28] As applied to the investment process, this statement is, perhaps, not particularly apt if the investment policy includes moral and social considerations but does not call upon the university affirmatively to *pursue* social goals. However, even the self-regulatory program referred to in the Basic Policy might be questioned in terms of its impact on university resources in relation to the benefits it produces. Any exercise of stockholder prerogatives on corporate responsibility questions will take administrative time that is costly and could be devoted to other university functions. Some efforts in the direction of corporate responsibility, if successful, may also involve a slight reduction of endowment return, but in amounts not easy to compute. It is even harder to quantify the societal benefits achieved through a university's social investment activities. Yet some attempt to deal with these issues is required in order to decide whether it is worth it for a university to undertake these activities in the first place.

This question is almost impossible to discuss in the abstract. In order to consider it adequately, one must know precisely what social investment approach is being proposed. Accordingly, further discussion of costs and benefits, and therefore of the efficiency objection, is postponed to the final pages of this chapter.

Nevertheless, our discussion of the competence objections permits us to set forth certain principles for investment (some of which we have encountered before). If a university's investment policy is to take moral and social considerations into account—

Social investment activities should be undertaken only if a university is able to devise a process that will yield reasonably skillful and competent decisions.

Criteria should be generated primarily by sources outside the academic community.

Criteria should be readily applicable to diverse and complex issues.

REFINEMENT OF THE BASIC POLICY

In the preceding pages, we have considered what appear to us to be the most serious challenges to the contention that a university ought to exercise, when carrying out its investment functions, the minimal responsibilities suggested by the Basic Policy. That discussion has yielded a series of "principles for investment" (some of which have recurred at several points). In the pages which follow, those principles for investment are set forth, together with a detailed outline of their implications for a university investment policy. (This outline is, in fact, a summary statement of the salient provisions of the Guidelines set forth in the Appendix.) Following this material, we shall expand on the way the Guidelines handle problems involving sales of securities.

Investment Principles and Guideline Implications

1. *The locus of decision-making should be separated from the academic enterprise.*

Final decision-making powers on all investment decisions are retained by the university's trustees. There is to be created, however, a University Investments Council which makes specific recommendations to the trustees. Its members include faculty and students (as well as alumni, a nonfaculty employee, and an administrator). All members of the council are to be appointed by the university president. Hence, the appointment procedures will be similar to those frequently employed for assignment to other administrative tasks that are advisory in nature. The significance of these provisions is that in investment management (even where social considerations are involved), just as in labor relations, fund raising, and similar activities, the faculty and the student body (comprising the principals in the academic enterprise) will not be—and in all probability will not be perceived to be—responsible for the university's decisions.

2. *Social investment activities should be undertaken only if a process which will yield reasonably skillful and competent decisions can be devised.*

An important rationale for the establishment of an advisory council is to tap what competence does reside in the student body, faculty, alumni, and other components of the university.

The Guidelines stress the desirability of appointing persons whose expertise lies in the subject matter areas in which social investment questions are likely to arise. Since the Guidelines specify that this council has considerable investigative and recommendatory responsibilities—and has available to it expert staff assistance—we are convinced that careful choice of council membership will aid the institution in making informed and thoughtful decisions. In addition, the fact that the trustees will taken an active role in reviewing the council's recommendations should significantly improve the quality of institutional determinations, since members of university boards normally have experience in financial matters and also are in an excellent position to anticipate the institutional effects of specific social investment decisions.

3. *Criteria should be generated primarily by sources outside the academic community.*

The proposed investment management policies focus upon corporate practices producing social injury, which, for the purposes of the guidelines, is defined as "particularly including activities which violate, or frustrate the enforcement of, rules of domestic or international law intended to protect individuals against deprivation of health, safety, or basic freedoms."

4. *Criteria should be readily applicable to diverse and complex issues.*

Application of the norms described under Principle 3 will not be effortless and uncomplicated. On some issues, for example, there may be competing—or even contradictory—public policies which are relevant. Even where the problem of competing policies does not arise, the norms are often broad and require interpretation. Finally it may be difficult to decide whether a particular stockholder proposal will be efficacious in reducing social injury. Nevertheless, these norms should give considerable guidance to decision-makers and are surely preferable to no norms at all. (See the hypothetical cases in chapter 4, where this assertion is, we believe, borne out.)

In addition, the fact that the guidlines do not favor divestment (instead, they require the exercise of shareholder voting and other rights on specific issues) relieves the university of making an exceedingly complex determination about the overall moral quality of a given company as a prelude to a to-sell-or-not-to-sell decision. Even in the unusual situation where divestment is called for under the Guidelines, the decision is made on the basis of the social injury caused by specific corporate activities, not on the basis of the company's overall moral purity. (For explanation of our emphasis on the exercise of shareholder rights, rather than disengagement from corporations thought to be causing social injury, see chapter 2, pp. 26, 53 and chapter 3, pp. 91-93; the latter pages also set forth our reasons for the limited amount of divestment activity the Guidelines do call for.)

5. *Decisions should be based on criteria generally acceptable to most of those within the academic community.*

In order to protect Principle 6 (below), the proposed policy does not call for universitywide referenda on social investment questions. And, in order to protect Principle 1, council members are not representatively elected. The twelve-member council, however, plus its ex officio members, will probably embrace many of the perspectives found within the university's constituencies. Moreover, the Guidelines do require that the council carefully assess the sentiments of the university community; the council is also encouraged to provide opportunity for expression of opinion in meetings open to all those who are interested.

6. *Plenary involvement of the entire university community in social investment decisions should be minimized or excluded.*

No provision is made for the holding of universitywide meetings at which investment recommendations are to be made. Opinions may vary on the appropriateness of such meetings for making judgments on moral and social issues, but regular plenary involvement to determine university policy could impair the Academic Context.

7. *Social investment decision-making should not become so time-consuming for the academic community that the educational process is impaired.*

The Guidelines describe procedures which do not involve more than a few members of the academic community. Moreover, one provision suggests that, where feasible, a research director be employed on a fulltime or parttime basis to gather, collate, and analyze materials relevant to the council's work. The university may make use of corporate annual reports, information provided by investment brokers, congressional committee findings, government agency reports (especially in the areas of environmental protection and fair employment), and the published material of interest groups and organizations. In addition, there is reason to believe that there are developing one or more well-qualified independent research organizations, such as the Council on Economic Priorities, to which the university may turn for reliable information; the guidelines suggest the utilization of such outside expertise.

8. *Except in unusual circumstances, the university should involve itself in social investment questions only if the issue is thrust upon it by other stockholders.*

The Guidelines specify that only in cases where there is discovered an instance of "grave" social injury, and where no other institutional or individual stockholder has taken effective steps to initiate or carry through correction of that injury, should the university ever adopt an initiating role as a shareholder (except for communications with management). Moreover, the Guidelines preclude the purchase of stock for the purpose of challenging or supporting corporate policies and bar any action on a shareholder proposal not related to the company's business (e.g., a proposal opposing the progressive income tax).

9. *Social investment decisions should not impair the fiscal ability of the university to perform its educational functions.*

The Guidelines provide that, with limited exceptions, maximum economic return—rather than social considerations—will be the basis for selection and retention of securities. The university will observe its social responsibilities through the way it exercises shareholder rights, but if the resulting modification of company policies significantly impairs the return from a security, it will be sold. Moreover, there is a general escape clause referred to under Principle 10.

10. *Provision should be made for the university to adjust its social investment policies in case of serious adverse consequences.*

In an extraordinary situation, where any action otherwise called for by the Guidelines would gravely damage the university's ability to carry out its purposes (where it would cause serious reprisals or deep internal divisions, for example), the university will not take such action.

A Further Note on Sales of Securities

Two provisions of the Guidelines that call for the sale of securities require further discussion. One of these provisions is set forth as an exception to the basic rule that securities are to be retained or sold only for economic return reasons—not for social injury reasons. The provision in question states that a security will be sold where the company is committing grave social injury and where all methods of correcting these practices have failed or appear doomed to failure.[29]

We have not recommended a more expansive use of such divestment; in other words, we have not proposed that divestment be employed as a firstline method for correcting corporate policies, for we think it improbable that it can have that effect. As explained in chapter 2, the "economics team" in our seminar concluded that the sale of holdings even several times as large as that likely to be owned by any one university would not have anything but a brief market price effect; accordingly, corporate managements would not be punished by such a sale and would have little reason to be deterred by the prospect of similar sales by other morally concerned institutions in the future. The result might be different if the sale were accompanied by public statements which had the capacity to build effective public pressures in favor of changed practices, but we doubt that universities will wish to engage in this process. In any event, if a university wished to engage in such a publicity campaign, it could do so without first divesting.

If divestment, then, is not an effective means of self-regulation (i.e., of correcting socially injurious practices), and if such self-regulation—rather than an effort to maintain institutional purity—is the point of this exercise, why should the Guidelines *ever* call for divestment, particularly since a loss in return (and some extra transaction costs) may thereby be incurred?[30]

One might defend such divestment on maximum economic return grounds. In other words, it may be argued that the stock should be sold under the conditions we have suggested (where correction of social injury cannot reasonably be anticipated), because in the long run an incorrigibly irresponsible company will fail badly; an adverse reaction from the public or the government will inevitably bring it down. Where this assertion supplies the motive for a university's social investment policies, it may also constitute a legal justification for such policies (as discussed in chapter 5). We cannot, however, truthfully state that considerations of maximum economic return inform our recommendations related to social injury; social or moral rather than fiscal concerns brought us to this study and to these suggested Guidelines. Moreover, we are not confident that the fiscal argument is always available. As our discussion in chapter 2 points out, the maximum economic return argument in favor of holding a morally clean portfolio depends on a predictive generalization which is yet to be proved and on a long-term investment intention which may not in fact correspond to a particular portfolio manager's time frame.

A candid defense, therefore, of the limited and residual divestment rule we have proposed is that it does not neatly fit into either the self-regulation or maximum return notions that inform our Guidelines. In fact, however, this divestment rule borrows a little from both notions. Thus, divestment may, in some cases, avert investment losses from a corporate calamity brought on by public or governmental hostility to a company's irresponsible behavior. And divestment may have some self-regulatory function; i.e., divestment by a university, if coupled with a statement informing the company of the reasons, may have some effect on management attitudes. Such action could bring home to the company a sense of outrage felt by at least one responsible constituent. Divestment, after all other corrective steps have failed, does remind us of the war movies in which the beleaguered infantryman, having exhausted his ammunition, finally hurls his rifle at the advancing hordes. It is, from his point of view, a terminal act which may help slightly; divestment seems to have similar characteristics.

The limited divestment rule also represents something else: it constitutes, as a distinctly untidy aspect of our approach, the vestigial trace of a purity notion which otherwise has been squeezed out of the Guidelines.[31] It is vestigial because it does not require that a university admire a company in order to hold its stock (we have not applied a love-it-or-leave-it policy); we do not even say that a university should decline dividends from a company which causes social harm. The recommended approach only says that if the harm caused is grave and if there is *nothing* the university as a shareholder—or anyone else—can do about it in any reasonably near future, then the university should disaffiliate.[32] It is an escape clause which spares an institution from being permanently locked into continuing association with a harmful enterprise because of the inexorable rigors of a maximum-return mandate.[33]

The second sale-of-security provision requiring discussion implements, rather than departs from, the basic maximum-return criterion for selection and retention of stocks. The provision in question precludes the selection or retention of a security "for the purpose of thereby encouraging or expressing approval of a company's activities. . . ." This provision therefore bars a university from retaining a security if the return it provides should decline to unacceptable levels as a result of the company's self-correction of socially injurious practices; i.e., the university sells the stock even though it helped to bring about the corrective action through the exercise of its shareholder rights.

Some readers may question this result on the ground that it is unfair for a shareholder to encourage reforms and then opt out of the corporation when those reforms prove quite costly. At the outset we note that it is unlikely that the portfolio managers would sell because of an apparently temporary or minimal reduction in earnings caused by self-regulatory expenditures. But a severe and predictably long-lived decline would result in such a sale. Our earlier discussion of divestment, however, suggests that even if many other investors sell at the same time, and if the price of the stock falls without rebound, that drop is not attributable to the sales alone, but primarily to the unfavorable economic data to which the sales draw the market's attention. The university cannot improve the underlying economic data by retaining its stock. At the most, holding the stock might marginally retard the nose-dive in market price. The university is not obliged to render such a kindness. The corporation's action in policing its own harmful conduct, in measuring up to minimum standards of self-regulation, is not an act of generosity toward the university or any other shareholder; the company's action therefore creates no reciprocal obligation on the university's part. The case might be different if the university had induced the corporation to undertake, at great cost, affirmative social welfare programs; but our Guidelines do not ask the university to press for such affirmative social activities. The case might also be different if the university had induced the company to undertake correction of social injury well ahead of all its competitors—a sacrificial pioneering effort which should, in some way, be requited; but our Guidelines preclude the university from seeking unilateral corporate action which causes "serious competitive disadvantage."

In any event, the Guidelines seek to avoid a chronology of corrective action followed by reduced earnings followed by sale of the stock. The Guidelines provide that where the university can anticipate that the correction of social injury "will, within the near future, have a sufficiently unfavorable impact on the company to cause the university to sell the securities under the maximum return criterion," the university will sell the stock before taking any corrective shareholder action. This provision, in turn, may be questioned on the ground that it will abort the university's participation in a proxy contest or litigation and thus undermine the university's ability to carry out a sustained program of corporate reform. But that is not the kind of program we have recommended in this book. The Basic Policy does not describe responsibilities that derive from a university's role as agent of social reform; the universities we deal with here have not admitted to such a role. Instead the Basic Policy articulates the duties that flow from the university's role as an economically motivated investor holding shares in certain companies. The "moral minimum" duties of the university-as-investor do not extend to companies in which the university no longer has an investment reason to participate—including a company which cannot provide an acceptable return once it has cleaned up its socially harmful practices.

Having defended the policy of selling stock in declining companies against a charge of "hit-and-run" unfairness, it remains to be said that there may conceivably be a situation where it is not the correction of social injury, but an unanticipated and peculiarly irrational chain of events triggered by the correction, that brings about a reduction in return. An example might be a case where a controversial (and courageous) act of corporate self-regulation brings on a damaging campaign of vandalism, boycott, or defamation against the company. This fairly remote contingency is simply not dealt with in our Guidelines; if it arose, and if the university's trustees believed that the company deserved symbolic support, despite reduced return, we assume that the trustees would consider departing from the Guidelines to deal with this extreme case. As we point out in the next section, extraordinary situations may require extraordinary measures; the Guidelines, we believe, will work well in most seasons, but perhaps not in all.

OBJECTIONS FROM ANOTHER PERSPECTIVE: IS THE BASIC POLICY TOO TIMID?

The Basic Policy as refined may well be criticized by those who consider such an approach too timid. This charge can be levied in respect to two aspects of the Policy.

First, it may be said that the issues on which the Policy focuses (e.g., those which relate to socially injurious corporate practices) constitute only a partial list of the corporate questions with which a university should be concerned as a responsible investor. In this connection we note that our Guidelines permit, but do not require, the university to vote on shareholder proposals dealing with social issues other than the regulation of social injury, i.e., issues relating to the internal structure of the corporation (such as shareholder democracy questions) or relating to affirmative social welfare programs (such as corporate charitable contributions). This option is limited, however, to voting on proposals made by other shareholders; it does not permit the university to initiate action with respect to such issues. Moreover, this option does not allow the university to vote on any proposal "which advances a position on a social or political question unrelated to the conduct of the company's business or the disposition of its assets" (such as a general resolution on police brutality or socialized medicine). In addition, we have provided an optional clause which would defer all action in such cases until the university has a chance to develop criteria dealing with these proposals.

Second, it may be asserted that the *means* for evidencing moral and social concern which the Guidelines specify are not sufficiently aggressive and hence do not allow a university an effective role as a responsible stockholder. As indicated previously, we have concluded that the exercise of stockholder rights is a more effective approach than divestment. But, with a few exceptions, the Guidelines do limit the university to a reactive rather than initiating role. They preclude the university from instituting proxy contests, derivative suits, and other stockholder activities except under very limited and carefully specified circumstances. They also preclude the special purchase or retention of stock for the purpose of either participating in or initiating ameliorative action. Finally, the university is permitted to retire from the field of corporate controversy (by, for example, selling its stock) when that controversy threatens severely to damage the Academic Context (financially or in other ways).

A more aggressive approach in relation either to issues or to means could be advanced on several grounds. In this section we will examine three arguments for such an approach.

Objection 1: As society's teacher and watchdog, it is incumbent upon a university to manifest in all its functions—including investment ones—its role as agent of a particular social perspective.

As we have seen, this view is incompatible with the prevailing views of a university's nature, its competence, and its role in society. In particular, it is dramatically inconsistent with the notion that a university itself should not erect any social or political orthodoxies. Although the university's role is currently a matter of intense discussion and serious dispute, we have indicated that the purpose of this essay is not to remake the university, but rather to discover whether some new initiatives in the area of social investment policy are possible or desirable without reversing the prevailing understandings about the nature of universities.*

Objection 2: The university should not limit itself to correction of social injury, but should manage its investments responsively to the social and moral views of the students and faculty, in order to avoid friction and mistrust not conducive to the maintenance of the Academic Context.

In the legal discussion found in chapter 5, we conclude that where university trustees base a social investment policy on the necessity of improving the interpersonal aspects of the university, this will provide an alternative legal basis for such a policy. Yet the fact that improvement of intrauniversity relations supplies a legal justification does not mean that it helps to define a satisfactory investment policy. Moreover, trustees guided by the view suggested here would be charged with the responsibility of determining how best to cool controversy involving the moral quality of the university's investments; such a judgment would have to take into account adverse reactions from those in the community who opposed a particular social determination, and also from those who opposed any social expression by the university. In

---

*Once again, we wish to stress that we do not here take a position on whether the existing institutional understandings are adequate or appropriate. Indeed, the authors differ on this question.

addition, a consistent anti-friction policy would require the trustees to make sure, on each occasion, that responding to a particular issue would not encourage later attempts to create friction as a
means of forcing the university to adopt other friction-resolving
policies. As a result of all these pushes and pulls, it is quite
possible that this rationale for social investment activity would
lead the trustees to avoid any decision that took moral and social
consequences into account. At the very least, such decisions
would be sporadic and wholly reactive.

In sum, although this objection does invoke a legal basis for
social investment action, it does not define a consistent or regu-
larly employable rationale for such activities. Some other, more
discriminating, basis is needed. The discussion of this objection
does remind us, however, that any kind of social investment
policy or decision should have substantial support from the constituencies of the university. This point, as earlier indicated, has
been incorporated into the Guidelines.

*Objection 3: The present social crisis so endangers human welfare
that the university as an investor should go beyond a "moral
minimum" response.*

This "world in flames" objection can be advanced on either of
two grounds: (a) because a world in flames is not one in which a
university can possibly maintain the ingredients of an Academic
Context, the university should actively and aggressively pursue
the amelioration of the social crisis if it is to be true to its own
mission; (b) in extraordinary crisis situations, no citizen (individual or institution) may limit himself to ordinary (minimal) responses. These grounds appear congruent: where the latter
ground applied, the crisis would be so pervasive and of such mag-
nitude that the university's own need to protect the Academic
Context would be coincident with society's need. Hence we shall
consider both contentions together.

At the outset we note that in times of dire emergency, investment policy would not be the first, or even an especially important, arena for ameliorative action. Hence, it is doubtful that
increasing the scope of the university's investment activities

would be the most efficacious way of helping a university to deal with such a situation. Other avenues—perhaps pressure for decisive governmental intervention or a radical shift in educational research or pedagogy (as happened, for example, during World War II)—would probably be employed.

Assuming that investment policy is, nevertheless, chosen as a mode of response to a grave crisis, we doubt that the Basic Policy would be excessively restrictive in regard to the issues it would permit the university to address. Social injury is not a static concept. Its content is contingent upon both the degree and nature of the society's problems. For example, in situations of dire emergency, new laws and rules would probably be promulgated to meet the needs created by that crisis. And because our definition of social injury is heavily (although not exclusively) dependent on public policy norms, the concept would expand accordingly.

Even if it is agreed that the Guidelines therefore permit a broad enough spectrum of issues to be addressed in a crisis, it could still be argued that they unduly restrict the modes of possible university action in an emergency setting. If this proved to be the case, however, the University Investments Council's request to the board of trustess for a temporary emendation or suspension of the Guidelines would, in all probability, be heeded. The Guidelines in their present form are not sacrosanct. They are calculated to permit the university to discharge its minimal responsibilities as an investor while, at the same time, maximizing awareness of the potential threats to the educational mission which uninhibited involvement in this, as in all social arenas, could cause. Extraordinary situations require extraordinary measures—and extraordinary measures entail risks of many sorts. The Guidelines do not purport to be adequate to such situations, even though they may help indicate what is being lost and gained as their provisions are being set aside.

For the university to enter upon such a state of total mobilization would require a wide consensus among the university constituencies that an emergency had arisen (whether or not society had reached this verdict). Obviously, that extraordinary consensus has not yet developed. Until it does, we do not discern the necessity for jettisoning the safeguards built into the Guidelines, particularly since, as we have noted, even a world in flames may not generate investment issues that the Guidelines fail to handle.

Our conclusion that the Basic Policy should not be faulted on grounds of timidity does not end our inquiry into the appropriateness of that Policy. Earlier we delayed discussion of the contention that the costs of any such policy would outweigh the benefits until we had developed and explained a specific proposal. That cost-benefit study must now be undertaken.

THE BASIC POLICY SUBJECTED TO COST-BENEFIT SCRUTINY

Results of the inquiry just completed seem to establish a presumption in favor of university adoption of a modified version of the Basic Policy. Although the Basic Policy must be qualified and specified to meet the special problems and purposes of the university, our analysis does not suggest that these problems or purposes vitiate the fundamental responsibility to avoid collaboration in social injury.

Where a "moral minimum" obligation is thus found to exist, we believe that those who wish not to honor it bear the burden of proof of making a contrary case. We reject the notion that, simply because such an obligation is newly recognized—and because it therefore is inconsistent with existing policies—the burden of proof rests on those who wish to alter the old policies.

Accordingly, we believe that those who contend that the immediate or long-term costs of the investment policies we have outlined are so high that they outweigh the benefits, and that these policies should not be adopted, have to overcome the presumption to which we have referred—the presumption in favor of honoring "moral minimum" responsibilities. Against this background, we turn to the cost-benefit considerations originally referred to in our discussion of the efficiency objection—considerations which are implicit in the question: should a university, in view of its limited resources, implement the social investment program we have set forth?

What makes cost-benefit analysis particularly difficult here is not simply the existence of many variables, but the necessity of weighing and comparing different classes of variables. An example will illustrate. Does the cost in time, money, and potential dysfunction which results from a university decision to participate in deterring the water polluting practices of a corporation generate greater benefit than sponsorship of a series of readings in contemporary French poetry? If the standard for this decision were simply "what best reduces the level of human suffering," there could be disagreement; but resolution of the disagreement might well be possible. If the standard were "what most contributes to human and social welfare," disagreement would undoubtedly be more strenuous. The difficulty is aggravated by the fact that the university must consider its social investment decisions under two disparate standards. The university's primary purpose (and hence its internal standard for cost-benefit analysis) is education, whereas its very existence depends on its involvement in economic activities which entail another set of responsibilities (e.g., those set forth in the Basic Policy), measured by a different standard.

The problems faced by the university are likely to differ, then, from those faced by a church or a broad-purpose foundation that is considering the inclusion of social criteria in its investment policies. The foundation whose charter purpose is to "serve the public welfare" must decide whether its aims are better served by allocating time and other resources to socially related investment programs or by spending the same resources on other worthy causes. Yet the foundation may be in the business, at least in part, of reducing social injury, and so the standard governing its business may not be different from the standard governing its investment policies. By contrast, the university's distinctive dilemma is this: the business of the university is, as Irving Kristol says, education; but that business brings with it an institutional obligation of a noneducational sort. How are these two imperatives to be compared?

The discussion that follows highlights this difficulty. Any costs that result from the policy we have outlined will be primarily (although not entirely) costs which divert resources of various sorts from the performance of the educational mission. On the other hand, the benefits are primarily those that will accrue to the members of the larger society because they may, as a result of these investment activities, suffer less social injury.

Costs

Costs have, in reality, been a major subject of this entire chapter, which has sought to clarify, reckon, and in some cases protect against any detrimental impact on the university (i.e., any cost) of adopting an investment policy built on the Basic Policy. Here we ask whether there are any costs hardy enough to survive the protective measures we have built into the proposed guidelines.

Two different (although related) types of costs must be considered: nonfiscal costs impairing the Academic Context and fiscal costs detracting from the strength of the academic enterprise.

Nonfiscal Costs. We have referred to the possible adverse impacts of a social investment program upon the Academic Context, including these effects: the creation of ideological orthodoxies affecting decision-making within the academic enterprise, the distraction of the academic enterprise through politicization, and the possibility of reprisal affecting free inquiry within the university. The investment principles cited previously seek to reduce to a minimal level the risk of such impacts. We believe it is reasonable to expect that these measures will be effective. In other words, we are not convinced that, if these Guideline provisions are adopted, the incorporation of the Basic Policy into university investment policy will impose a cost in terms of the Academic Context.

Indeed, the existing policies that do not reflect social or moral considerations may impose a greater cost. Since trust in a university's administrative policies—and in its administrators—helps to avoid the tumult which hurts the Academic Context, university decision-making that appears to be insensitive to student and faculty views may be counterproductive. (See chapter 5, pp. 156-64.) It is of significance, in this connection, that the faculty and student bodies of at least one major university (Harvard) believe that university investment policies should take social considerations into account (see p. 104); similarly, the faculty of Cornell University, in 1968, voted 522 to 166 in favor of including "moral and social concerns . . . in determining the university's investment policy."

One other nonfiscal cost should be considered. As a result of its initial adoption or its implementation in particular cases, the policy we propose might be viewed as a precedent for more aggressive social or political action by the university in the future, with either of the following unfavorable results: the university will not undertake such expanded activity, thus disappointing the high expectations of students or others, or the university will meet these expectations by embarking on a course inappropriate for a university. We do not view this problem lightly: indeed, much of this report is intended to clarify precisely what we do and do not propose and thus to minimize the danger of misinterpretation. We believe that if a similar explanation accompanied a university's decision to adopt and implement this policy, the cost we are discussing would not be significant.

Fiscal Costs. Implementation of the policy set forth in the Guidelines would involve three possible fiscal costs:

(a) Some administrative expense—both indirect (in terms of the time of existing personnel) and direct (travel and telephone expenses in obtaining information and possibly the salary of a full-time or parttime research director and/or secretarial help if these services are engaged).

(b) Reduction in endowment return. We believe that this reduction would be minimal, in view of the Guideline provisions requiring that most buy-and-sell decisions be based on maximum economic return criteria and that securities be sold if the correction of social inquiry significantly impairs the return. (See p. 192, note 30, for additional discussion of this potential cost.)[34]

(c) Reduced contributions from private donors or governmental bodies that are adversely affected or offended by particular social investment decisions. This possibility is reduced by the prospect that many or most alumni will favor such an investment program, as explained below, and by the prospect that full explanation of the policy will minimize reprisals.

In evaluating the significance of both fiscal and nonfiscal costs, two other considerations are germane. First, the available evidence suggests that university constituencies approve of investment policies which specifically include social considerations. Recent studies of Harvard University's faculty, students, and alumni reveal that the majority of all those constituencies support (either in principle or in specific instances) such policies. A poll of the alumni, the constituency commonly thought to be the most reticent to accept changes in university practice, revealed that the majority of those responding answered in the affirmative to the question: "In general, should the Corporation consider public policy as well as income production in planning and voting its investment portfolio?" And the respondents from two recent Harvard classes ('63 and '66) unanimously voted *Yes*. [35] Harvard faculty and students appear to have concurred in the alumni view by virtue of their majority support of the resolutions proposed by the Project on Corporate Responsibility to General Motors in the spring of 1970. Where an institution's participating and supporting constituencies favor implementation of a policy, it seems likely that the cohesiveness of the institution is strengthened and its ability to attract additional support is enhanced. This argument is not put forward as an affirmative reason for adopting the Guidelines we propose; it does, however, suggest a possible offset to any other costs that might be attributed to these policies.

In the second place, our Guidelines provide, as we have indicated, that in any case where the actual functioning of the academic enterprise appears to be threatened by serious reprisals or deep internal divisions resulting from social investment activities, the university will either modify its activities or, if necessary, temporarily retire from the field. To those who object that this safety clause avoids responsibility, it may be pointed out that if, as a result of such reprisals or divisions, the quality of educational activity were critically impaired, there would be no university and, hence, no responsibility. To those who fear that the safety clause might not be invoked until the damage was done, we would point out that this clause is quickly and easily administrable. Therefore, it is likely to protect the university from running as great a risk of adverse unintended consequences as the risk incurred in many of the university's other activities, (e.g., investing in securities in an unpredictable stock market, or educating a potentially volatile student body).

In summary, although the administrative costs involved in the implementation of the proposed policy can be determined (and regulated in advance), the other costs (fiscal and nonfiscal) cannot easily be predicted. There is reason to believe, however, that these costs would not be substantial.

Benefits

The primary benefit against which the costs of the proposed investment policy should be weighed is the reduction of social injury. The prospects for such reduction depend in part on the mode of action the university pursues.

We have discussed in chapter 2 the question of the effectiveness of shareholder action, particularly the exercise of shareholder rights to initiate and/or vote on shareholder resolutions and to raise questions (formally or informally) with corporate managements. Since certain aspects of these shareholder rights are now in the process of being clarified in the federal courts and because the effort to exercise these powers for the purpose of reducing social injury is a fairly new phenomenon, it is difficult to make a confident estimate of their efficacy. What evidence is available, however, suggests that their use can have positive results.[36] There is little history relating to shareholder litigation dealing with social issues, and, accordingly, it is not possible to predict the efficacy of such activity.

Divestment of stock for the purpose of influencing deleterious corporate policy appears, on the basis of the evidence available to us, to be the activity least likely to deter social injury. Nevertheless, divestment does remove an investor from a position of apparent acquiescence in socially injurious activity—a position that might result from continued stock ownership where correction has proved impossible.

Our proposed Guidelines follow these tentative conclusions about effectiveness. We emphasize employment of shareholder voting and communicating prerogatives, leave open the possibility of litigation in an exceptional case, and propose sale of stock for reasons other than inadequate return only when it appears that stockholder activities to reduce social injury will not meet with success. Evidence that other investors (institutional and individual) are adopting somewhat similar policies suggests that the approach we propose may acquire additional effectiveness in the future, from the force of numbers.[37]

There are some observers who believe that for the same expenditure of administrative time, academic talent, and perhaps money, the university can achieve a greater benefit in furtherance of any particular social objective by mounting a concerted scholarly program than by seeking to exercise shareholder rights. Thus, if the objective is to reduce water pollution, a university interdisciplinary research task force can achieve more than can be brought about through seeking to correct the polluting practices of corporations in the university's portfolio.

We doubt, in the first place, that the costs of the modest social investment program we have proposed are at all comparable to the costs of such an interdisciplinary academic effort. Moreover, apart from the possibility that the two approaches might compete for the same funds, we doubt that they would be competitive in any other way. In other words, if the investment approach we have outlined would impose only minimal costs, there is no reason why the research task force approach could not be attempted at the same time.

In any event, the argument we have just cited proceeds from a faulty premise; it assumes that the pursuit of social objectives is the point of the policies we have proposed. But as we have seen, the purpose of these policies is not to use the investment portfolio to pursue social goals; the purpose is to make sure that necessitous economic activity does not compel the university to participate in social injury. If that approach is, as we have contended, one that is required to fulfill a "moral minimum" obligation, it would take a very convincing case indeed to justify the abandonment of the investment policies we have outlined on the ground that some other university effort will outweigh, in social effectiveness, the failure to honor the "moral minimum" obligation.

Summary

This analysis of the costs and benefits is, at best, inconclusive. As we suggested at the outset, the examination involves the weighing of apples and oranges. It now appears that the weight of each fruit is itself difficult to determine. We believe, however, that if there are any indicators at all, they point in the direction of the benefits outweighing the costs. The potential costs appear to be minimal and, in any event, can be averted by resorting to the safety clause, which allows the university to avoid serious threats. It appears reasonable to anticipate significant social benefits on the basis of the limited experience investors have had in initiating or participating in similar social investment activities. As more experience with the employment of the Guidelines accumulates and as the interaction between corporations and their socially concerned stockholders increases, some of the unknowns in the equation will become clearer. University boards of trustees and advisory councils should continue to accumulate this evidence and to evaluate social investment policies in the light of what they find.

Perhaps the most important conclusion which can be drawn from this analysis is that at the present time it will be difficult for either supporters or opponents of the proposed Guidelines to buttress their position by appeal to an unambiguous cost-benefit table. It follows that the presumption for which we argued at the beginning of this section has not been overcome, nor, in fact, has it been seriously challenged. In the absence of a respectable showing that costs outweigh benefits, the "moral minimum" obligation should prevail.

In an address to alumni on Alumni Day at Yale, cited earlier, Kingman Brewster spoke of the "terrible tension at the moment between the imperative of university neutrality and the imperative of university morality." This tension comes to focus in many issues, only one of which is addressed in this report. We hope that the foregoing discussion will point the way to a constructive resolution of this tension in relation to the deployment of a university's investment funds.

4. Hypothetical Cases Illustrating the Suggested Guidelines*

CASE A

The university owns common stock of Company A, a manufacturing firm selected by the portfolio managers for maximum return reasons. A student asks the University Investments Council to "do something" about the contribution of Company A to the pollution of certain inland waterways through discharge of industrial wastes. The research director of the council obtains information on the question from the state agency charged with pollution control, from a citizen's environmental action group in the region, and from the management of Company A. After consideration of the evidence, the council finds that Company A has recently made considerable efforts to bring itself into compliance with applicable (though inadequate) state and federal laws and regulations; that further improvement in waste treatment would require massive capital expenditures that would leave Company A in a disadvantageous position with respect to its competitors, whose pollution record is not significantly better. The council concludes that industrywide government action is needed to correct the "grave social injury" caused by the pollution practices of several competing companies. Accordingly, under paragraph B4(b) of the Guidelines, the council recommends that the trustees communicate with Company A's management to urge it to take the lead in bringing about industrywide efforts to eliminate such pollution, and that further shareholder action be deferred pending the outcome of these communications. The trustees adopt this recommendation.

---

*In every case except cases G, I, and K, the corporate conduct described in the case is based on what we understand to have been the actual conduct of one or more American companies in the recent past; however, the companies on which we based these cases did not necessarily undergo the history of shareholder protest we have set forth in most of the cases.

When paragraph numbers are cited, the reference is to the proposed Guidelines set forth in the Appendix.

CASE B

Company B, whose common stock is held by the university, is a major manufacturer of certain antipersonnel bombs used in Vietnam which, according to certain stockholders of Company B, are notable for their wide range and erratic burst patterns and the resulting inability of American forces to confine their impact to military personnel. These bombs are also alleged to inflict an extraordinary degree of suffering and dismemberment on the persons—largely civilians—in the villages where these weapons are used. The group of shareholders succeeds in requiring Company B's management to include in the management's proxy materials a resolution which would amend the company's charter so as to preclude further manufacture of these weapons.

Upon receipt of these proxy materials, the research director of the council collects various printed reports and consults two reputable military journalists concerning the accuracy of these allegations and also calls on the management of Company B and the Defense Department for further information. The research director also calls on several members of the university's law school faculty and Company B's counsel to comment on the allegation that the use of these weapons constitutes a violation of the principles of law enunciated in Articles 25 and 27 of Hague Convention IV and Articles 3.1 and 18 of the Geneva Convention (1949), and as reflected in the Charter of the International Military Tribunal at Nuremburg. After reviewing this information, the council concludes that, quite apart from the validity of the Vietnam involvement, use of these weapons imposes an illegal degree of harm on nonenemy civilian populations and that Company B is a participant in this illegal action, which inflicts "grave social injury."

The council has also been informed by the portfolio managers that these weapons contracts are sufficiently important to Company B's income so that passage of the proposed charter amendment would predictably lower the return from Company B's stock below that which could be anticipated from other industrial stocks. Under paragraph B4(a)(ii) of the Guidelines, this prediction would require sale of the stocks in lieu of shareholder action if the reduced return were anticipated "within the near future." Because, however, it is not expected that the shareholder proposal will pass "within the near future"—or that Company B will soon discontinue manufacture of antipersonnel bombs—paragraph B4(a)(ii) is not invoked.* Accordingly, the council recommends voting the stock in favor of the shareholders' proposal. The trustees adopt this recommendation by a divided vote.

CASE C

A recent alumnus asks the university to give him its proxies for the voting of Company C's stock so that he may obtain addition votes for a resolution which the alumnus, as a shareholder of Company C, is planning to introduce at the next annual meeting. The resolution would declare the company to be opposed to the continuation of the Vietnam War. Because the proposed resolution does not deal with social injury imposed by the company's own business activities, it is not one for which the university may vote under paragraph B2(b) of the Guidelines, and the alumnus is so informed.

CASE D

A member of the council invites the council's attention to the fact that a Southern bank in which the university holds shares (traded over-the-counter) has recently joined with other banks in lending money on preferential terms to a number of segregated private academies that were started by white parents in response to the recent desegregation court decrees. After obtaining information about the role of these academies from the United States Commission on Civil Rights and the Southern Regional Council

---

*If it were concluded that the manufacture of these bombs could not be halted "within a reasonable period of time," then paragraph B4(a)(i) of the Guidelines would require sale of the securities without taking shareholder action. Here, however, no such finding of ultimate futility has been made by the council.

and having asked the banks to explain the terms of these loans (no answer was received), the council concludes that the loans were made for the purpose of fostering the continuation of a dual school system, thus frustrating the Supreme Court's decisions and representing a "grave social injury" calling for shareholder action. The council also finds that the prospects of effecting any change in the bank's policies are extraordinarily remote because of the extreme unlikelihood that many other shareholders of this particular bank will vote against these practices, and because of the doubtful legal basis for any shareholder litigation to correct these practices. Accordingly, the council recommends sale of the securities, based on paragraph B4(a)(i) of the Guidelines which provides for sale where it is found that

> it is unlikely that, within a reasonable period of time, the exercise of shareholder rights by the University (together with any action taken by others) will succeed in modifying the company's activities sufficiently to eliminate at least that aspect of social injury which is grave in character. . . .

The trustees accept this recommendation.

CASE E

A faculty member reports that Company E, an electric utility, is engaging in "red-lining" slum areas in the city in which it operates, i.e., according these areas blanket treatment as high-risk regions in which all customers must make substantial deposits before obtaining service and in which service is terminated with special haste when payments are late. The research director ascertains the truth of this report by visiting the headquarters of Company E. The council concludes that the hardship thus visited on many individually non-"risky" residents of the slum areas and, more important, the angry feeling of victimization this policy induces on the part of the entire slum sub-population, add up to a case of present or potential "grave social injury" warranting shareholder action. The investment managers report that it is not at all clear that an end of red-lining would reduce the return from this investment. The council recommends that the trustees direct the university officers to communicate the university's concern, as a shareholder, about this practice. The trustees adopt this recommendation.

CASE F

A student suggests to the council that the university acquire some tobacco stocks for the purpose of taking shareholder action to make the tobacco companies expand their required practice of issuing public warnings about the danger of smoking. The council rejects the proposal because it is inconsistent with paragraph B1(b) of the Guidelines, precluding purchase of securities for the purpose of contesting corporate policies. The student is so informed.

CASE G

Company G, which manufactures computers, sells some of its products to the Egyptian government for use in connection with the installation of missile-launching equipment in Egyptian territory. A student asks the president of the university to sell its stock in Company G because of these actions. The question is referred to the council, which discusses the issue of the threat to peace represented by the installation of the missiles. Eventually, the council declines to act on the student proposal, for the council does not itself feel competent to express a view on the implications and "social injury" consequences of the Egyptian action. Moreover, the council finds it particularly difficult in this case to ascertain what "opinions . . . appear to be held by substantial numbers of persons within the university community"—a factor it must take into account under paragraph C3(e) of the Guidelines. Accordingly, it declines to recommend action to the trustees, and so advises the student.

CASE H

A faculty member who has recently spent some time in South

Africa writes to the council about the university's ownership of shares in Company H, a manufacturing firm with a plant and sales-and-service office in South Africa. The faculty member asks the university to respond to the fact that the company is complying with the Job Reservation Act, which, as construed by the Labor Ministry, requires that whites be hired first and that non-whites not be hired for any job which would lead to racial mixing on the same work level, and prohibits the employment of non-whites in supervisory positions over whites. The faculty member further reports that, although skilled labor shortages have caused the government to overlook the upgrading of job opportunities for non-whites by some companies in South Africa, Company H (along with a number of other companies) has rigidly adhered to the official interpretation of the Job Reservation Act. The council's research director asks Company H to comment on this report; Company H replies simply that it is company policy scrupulously to obey the law in every country in which it operates.

The council first reaches the conclusion, after consulting with faculty and student members of the university's law school, that the South African laws violate principles of international law embodied in Article 23 of the U.N. Declaration of Human Rights and Article 55 of the U.N. Charter, and specifically interpreted in several U.N. Security Council and General Assembly resolutions condemning the South African *apartheid* laws and recommending economic sanctions against the South African government. The council also concludes that Company H has failed to do what it reasonably could, either quietly or openly, to end its own discriminatory employment based on these laws. In reaching this conclusion the council relies on the suggestions for corporate action contained in a document prepared by the South Africa Institute of Race Relations. The council finds that Company H has imposed "grave social injury" on its present and potential non-white employees, which requires some action on the university's part.

The council then considers the following possible courses of action: sale of the stock (recommended by a student group which appears before the council); shareholder action to try to make

Company H discontinue its South African operations (recommended by the complaining faculty member); shareholder action to try to make Company H upgrade the job opportunities for nonwhites (even though this entails the risk of Company H's expulsion from South Africa).

Considering the sale-of-stock option, the council consults with the university's investment managers. They report that Company H is one of the more promising holdings in the portfolio, and that it will continue to be so even if it should discontinue its South African operations (which are a small fraction of its total business). The council thereupon rejects the proposal for the sale of stock, following paragraphs B1(a) and B4(a) of the Guidelines, which permit a sale based on nonprofit factors only where the correction of social injury will significantly impair the return from the stock (which the investment managers have said is not the case), or where the social injury does not appear susceptible of correction (the council here is not persuaded of such a prognosis).

After considerable debate, the council finds that it is divided about the economic impact that the second alternative—seeking Company H's removal—would have on the nonwhite population of South Africa. Accordingly, the council chooses the third option—shareholder action to correct Company H's employment policies.*

The council next weighs various forms of shareholder action to correct Company H's employment policies; it decides to recommend that the university trustees first seek to persuade management to alter these policies, and, failing such efforts, that the trustees propose a resolution for the next shareholders' meeting, attempt to place the resolution on the management ballot, and seek support for its adoption. (The council recommends, however, pursuant to paragraph B3(d) of the Guidelines, that if

---

*Here, as in the other hypothetical cases, neither council nor trustee decisions necessarily represent the authors' own views—a fact we reiterate here because the selection of the third course of action would not be our unanimous choice. One of us would prefer the second option. For all of us, it is a close question.

another shareholder starts such a campaign, the university should not take the initiative but should lend its support to the other shareholder.)

Before notice of its action is forwarded to the trustees, however, the council receives information that, at the forthcoming annual meeting, another shareholder of Company H will introduce a shareholder resolution urging management to discontinue its manufacturing operations in South Africa, and that this shareholder has secured the inclusion of his resolution in the management proxy materials. In the supporting statement, the shareholder states that his primary motivation for putting the issue before the other shareholders is that the corporation's manufacturing facilities would, in the event of a national emergency, be converted to the production of weaponry to be used for the defense of the existing regime.

The council decides to delay forwarding its recommendation to the trustees and to request the research director to develop facts relevant to determining whether the new information should affect the council's earlier decision. The research director reports that the newspaper of the governing political party in South Africa has stated that Company H's installations could be "rapidly turned over to the production of weapons and other strategic requirements" in the event of an emergency. He notes that the Security Council of the United Nations has called upon member states to cease the sale and shipment of arms, armaments, and military vehicles to South Africa and that the United States government has complied with the Security Council's request.

After considerable debate, the University Investments Council determines that, although no international body has specifically proscribed the maintenance of installations of this type by member states, the corporation's operations in South Africa do frustrate the public policy norms reflected in the Security Council's embargo action, and thus constitute "social injury" under paragraph A2(e) of the Guidelines. The council reverses its earlier position (which rejected the notion of withdrawal) and recommends to the trustees that the university vote for the shareholder resolution on withdrawal from South Africa. The trustees adopt the recommendation.

CASE I

Company I manufactures a rather unique, patent-protected electrical product which gives it something of a monopoly position in a small sector of the electrical industry. A member of the council reads that Company I is considering a substantial price increase, despite recent healthy profit margins and an absence of recent wage increases. The council member asks the council to consider asking the university to introduce a shareholder resolution pointing out the inflationary effect of such a failure to use pricing self-restraint, as requested by the federal government. (This case arises long before the mandatory wage-price freeze imposed August 15, 1971.)

In order to recommend initiation of such shareholder action under paragraph B3 of the Guidelines, the council must find that the company policies impose grave social injury. After consulting a number of economists with varying views and after considering the recent slowdown in the rate of inflation, the council finds that it is divided on the question of whether the impact of any price increases that Company I is likely to make would constitute grave social injury.

It seems clear, however, that another shareholder will present a resolution on this matter to the next annual meeting and will solicit proxies in support of the resolution. A university vote for a resolution initiated by another shareholder would not require the "grave" finding, and the council is agreed that, on the basis of what it now knows, *some* degree of social injury would result from a price increase.

Accordingly, the council rejects the proposal that the university initiate shareholder action and tables the question of voting for the shareholder resolution until the wording of the resolution is received, at which time the council will solicit the views of the company's management before making a final recommendation.

CASE J

An alumnus sends the council a newspaper clipping reporting that Company J, a leading manufacturing corporation in which the university owns shares, is negotiating with the Soviet government for a contract pursuant to which the company would build an automobile assembly plant in the U.S.S.R. The alumnus contends that this contract would "give aid and comfort to the implacable enemies of the United States" and should be the subject of an immediate protest by the university to Company J's management. He states that the contract would frustrate the norms of American domestic law reflected in the Agricultural Trade Development and Assistance Act of 1954 (discouraging trade with the U.S.S.R., although not prohibiting this assembly plant construction), the Communist Control Act of 1954, the Internal Security Act of 1950, and various other pieces of legislation.

The council concludes that the legal norms cut both ways, for various treaties signed with the U.S.S.R. and ratified by the Senate reflect a legislative interest in peaceful cooperation between the two countries. Moreover, a majority of the council finds that, apart from legal norms, there is no social injury that will result from this activity. Two members of the Council disagree on this point, stating that the possibility that the plant may be converted to the production of military vehicles means that it may contribute materially "to further acts of repression in Czechoslovakia and elsewhere." By a 9-to-2 vote (one member abstaining because of his family connections with the leadership of Company J), the council declines to recommend action to the trustees. The alumnus is so informed.

At a subsequent meeting of the council, the two dissenting members ask for a reconsideration of the case on the ground that in a similar case (see Case H), the council had recommended that the university support a shareholder resolution calling for the suspension of a corporation's manufacturing operations in South Africa because they contributed to the military capability of that government. In rebuttal, other council members argue that the cases are not comparable: there is no public policy analogous to the Security Council's ban on foreign sales of arms to South Africa; and the defense capability of the U.S.S.R. would not be materially increased by the construction of the assembly plant. Hence, these members argue, the case in question is sufficiently

different to call for a different result. A second vote reveals that
no council member has altered his position.

CASE K

Company K, which manufactures surgical and hospital supplies,
has developed a surgical device which makes it possible for physicians to perform safe and inexpensive office abortions. In an
attempt to insure that this product is not used for illegal operations, Company K makes this equipment available only on a lease
basis; a condition of the continuation of the lease is that the
physician must submit to certain audit and office inspection procedures to determine whether he has been performing abortions
in contravention of the laws of the state in which he is located.

These safeguards fail to impress a shareholder of Company K,
who proposes that the following resolution be adopted at the
next annual meeting:

Whereas, the performing of abortions in cases not posing a
threat to the mother's life is, in the eyes of God, a murder of
the unborn child, now be it

Resolved, that the Certificate of Incorporation of the Company
be amended to include the following clause: "Notwithstanding
the powers hereinbefore set forth, the Company shall not manufacture or produce any equipment or other item which is designed for, or principally employed in, the planned termination
of pregnancies.

The shareholder's proposal is included in the materials sent to
the university by Company K's management; the management
recommends a vote against the resolution.

The council finds that the statutory laws governing abortion are
not violated or frustrated by Company K's activity, in view of the
company's safeguards against illegal use. The council debates the
question of whether social injury is nevertheless caused because
Company K's product facilitates the denial of life to the unborn
child and because, in some states, the equipment can be used even
though the mother's life is not in jeopardy. Through notices in

the university newspaper and the alumni magazine the council invites members of the university community to present their views. At length, the council, by a divided vote, decides that the social injury caused by denying women the ability to have abortions outweighs the opposing claim of social injury. It recommends to the trustees that they vote against the shareholder's resolution.

The trustees, considering the depth and strength of the opinions received by the council, reject the council's recommendation on the ground that, in the language of paragraph B4(d) of the Guidelines, such a course of conduct "is likely to impair the capacity of the university to carry out its educational mission (... by causing deep divisions within the University community)." The trustees decide not to vote on the proposition in question. The council is so informed.

CASE L

The federal government has brought a law suit under the Civil Rights Act of 1964 against Company L, a major metals producer, and against the union of its employees, alleging discrimination against black employees in job assignments, training, and promotions at a major plant in the South. The Justice Department explains that the suit was brought after the Equal Employment Opportunity Commission had found that such discrimination existed and had failed to obtain voluntary compliance. The company has denied the allegation, pointing to its affirmative efforts to recruit and provide training and advancement opportunities for black employees.

An employee of the university writes to the trustees to ask that the university introduce a resolution at the next annual meeting of the company condemning the management for its discriminatory practices. Pursuant to paragraph C3(g) of the Guidelines, the question is referred to the council.

In the early stages of its discussion, the council considers the question of how it is to determine the difference between a discriminatory practice (which would clearly "violate or frustrate" a norm of domestic law and thus constitute clear social injury) and a failure to take forceful compensatory action in the employment field (which would present a more doubtful case of social injury). The council also wonders what weight it should attach to the findings of the Equal Employment Opportunity Commission.

The council, however, does not find it necessary to resolve these questions at this time, for it concludes that the pendency of the Justice Department's suit forecloses any initiating action by the university in the light of paragraph B3(d), which states that "the university will not play an initiating role to any extent beyond that which is necessary to ensure that appropriate corrective action is commenced. . . ." The employee is so informed.

CASE M

In advance of the annual meeting of Company M, a large coal producing company, the university receives a proxy solicitation from a conservation group which holds shares in Company M. The group plans to nominate and vote for a noted professor of forestry to serve on Company M's board of directors, in place of one member of the management slate of nominees. The proxy materials explain that Company M has engaged in very aggressive strip-mining activities in a particular county in Ohio, which have "despoiled and devastated the land beyond any realistic hope of reclamation." The materials quote the Regional Planning Commission as stating that the strip-mining severely disturbs the ecological balance of the area and precludes development for housing and commercial purposes. The materials state that the point of nominating the professor to the board is to "ventilate" Company M's deliberations on this subject.

The council solicits the views of the company, which characterizes the opposition as "sentimentalism" and also points out that the farmers who sell their land to the strip-miners are marginal operators for whom the sale represents economic salvation; further, they point to the nation's severe shortages of coal.

After consulting faculty members and students working in the fields of forestry and geology, the council concludes that Company M's strip-mining represents an unnecessarily destructive way to develop the nation's fuel resources and that it ignores the near-term and long-term well being of the majority of the residents of the county and surrounding territories. There is no existing state statute on the subject in Ohio (although efforts are being made in this direction); nor does federal legislation provide a legislative norm against which to view Company M's activities. Although the Guidelines, in paragraph A2(e), say that social injury activities "particularly include activities which violate, or frustrate the enforcement of" legal norms, the council decides that it may properly make a finding of social injury in this case. In so doing, the council is mindful that the university is not being asked to help compel Company M to desist from strip-mining, but only to help install a director who can raise environmental questions within the company. Accordingly, the council recommends that the trustees give the university's proxy to the conservationist group for the limited purpose of voting for its nominee.

The trustees, by a divided vote, accept the council's recommendation.

CASE N

Three shareholder proposals appear on the proxy materials mailed by the management of Company N, a producer of petroleum products and pesticides, for the 1971 annual meeting. One resolution would amend the company's by-laws to provide for cumulative voting in the election of shareholders (theoretically permitting a substantial minority group of shareholders to bunch its votes to elect a director). Another resolution would establish a ceiling of $200,000 per annum on all executive salaries. The third resolution would require the annual report to the stockholders to contain a detailed description of all legal or governmental proceedings involving any of the company's products. (The statement accompanying the third proposal explains that reports have been received by the U.S. Environmental Protection Agency to the effect that a pesticide produced by the company, when handled by nonprofessional purchasers without proper training and equipment, has caused or may cause liver damage, lung disease, and perhaps blindness.) The management recommends a "No" vote on all three resolutions.

One of the council members contends that the council should decline to act on all three resolutions for the following reasons. All three questions, he states, involve nonprofit considerations—shareholder democracy in the first and third cases and distributional justice in the second case—but none involves the correction of social injury. The council member points out that paragraph B2(d) states that the university "may, but need not, vote on" proposals which are related to social questions but *not* related to the correction of company-caused social injury. He also points out that criteria for handling such cases have not yet been developed pursuant to paragraph D3 and adds that he does not believe that the council should deal with such cases on an ad hoc basis.

The council agrees with the member's position with respect to the first and second resolutions (cumulative voting and executive compensation) but concludes that the third resolution (information on legal proceedings) will assist in efforts to correct social injury. Accordingly, the council recommends to the trustees that the university cast no vote on the first two questions and a "Yes" vote on the third. The trustees accept this recommendation.

CASE O

In the proxy materials distributed by Company O, a manufacturing company, there appear two diametrically opposed shareholder proposals relating to corporate charitable gifts.

One resolution would amend the by-laws to prohibit all charitable contributions; the other recommends to the board of directors that the company give the full amount permitted to be deducted for federal income tax purposes (5 per cent of taxable income). The first stockholder argues that the directors are spending "our money" to support "liberal causes in which not all of us believe, such as the National Urban League." The second shareholder argues that "society's unmet needs are so enormous that our company should play a far greater part. . . ."

Although these resolutions relate to nonprofit factors, the council concludes that they do not relate to the correction of company-caused social injury and, accordingly, need not be acted upon, as explained in the discussion of Case N, above. Nor have criteria been developed for dealing with these cases Nevertheless, the council concludes that a diminution in corporate charitable giving would be unfortunate, for in forcing greater reliance on governmental support for private charitable institutions, it might chill expression of diverse points of view. The council believes the university should act on this proposal despite the absence of over-all criteria. Accordingly, it recommends a "No" vote on the first resolution (prohibiting all contributions). With respect to the second resolution, the council finds that Company O has given charitable gifts slightly in excess of the national average for corporations (approximately one per cent of taxable income); the council is not clear by what criteria a corporation should be judged on its failure to contribute at a higher level, and, accordingly recommends abstention on this resolution pending further study of the issues involved. The trustees accept these recommendations.

CASE P

Company P, a manufacturing company in which the university owns shares, has recently announced that it will move its corporate headquarters from a large city to a suburb approximately 40 miles away. The suburb has no rental housing (except for one luxury apartment complex) and virtually no sales housing with a market value of less than $35,000. All of the remaining undeveloped land is zoned either for nonresidental purposes or for two-acre lots (with multiple dwellings prohibited); inexpensive housing cannot feasibly be built on land zoned in this manner.

Roughly 1,000 persons are employed at corporate headquarters, of whom approximately 700 are not executives and earn less than $15,000 per year. Of these 700, approximately 100 are minority group employees, most of whom have relatively unskilled jobs and therefore earn less than $8,000 per year.

Because of housing costs, many of the 700 nonexecutives will find it impossible to live in the vicinity of new suburban headquarters, and most of these persons will also find it too expensive to commute there from their present homes. This result will follow almost universally for the minority group employees; moreover, if their jobs are taken by residents of the suburban town or the neighboring communities, these residents will almost surely be white, in view of the present demographic pattern found in the area.

This situation is brought to the council's attention by the university's Black Student Union. The council is informed that this matter is the subject of a complaint before federal and state agencies, alleging that the corporate relocation, under these circumstances, amounts to employment discrimination in violation of civil rights statutes and in breach of the company's contracts with the federal government. It appears, however, that because of the wording of the statutes and regulations governing these proceedings, they are unlikely to lead to enforcement measures. The council therefore decides to investigate the possibility of university action. It finds that Company P's actions will not only inflict injury on its minority employees but will also contribute to city-suburb, black-white polarization in metropolitan regions. It also finds that Company P has made no effort to overcome the suburban town's zoning rules, effectively barring low income housing. The council therefore recommends that the trustees communicate with Company P's management and ask it not to proceed with the headquarters move until there is some reasonable prospect of adequate housing for minority and other low income employees.

CASE Q

The proxy materials distributed by the management of Company Q, a railroad, include a shareholder proposal calling on the company to refuse to buy diesel fuel from any oil company whose tankers have been guilty of an oil spill in coastal waters.

The council finds that Company Q's purchases of fuel from such companies do not constitute social injury, for as defined in paragraph A2(e), that term does not include "doing business with other companies . . . engaged in socially injurious activities." Moreover, the prevention of spills, the Council finds, is too complicated to be achieved by a simple act of will on the part of an oil company; accordingly, encouraging a boycott of such a company would be an ineffective or unreasonable method for correcting social injury, and such a method is not to receive the university's support under the second sentence of paragraph B2(c).

The council recommends a vote against the proposal, and the trustees accept the recommendation.

CASE R

Company R, a major producer of soft beverages, has been accused by a Senate committee of failing to provide safe, sanitary, or humane housing for the migrant workers who harvest certain crops used in producing its beverages. On the basis of these complaints, a boycott of the company's products has begun in several cities. Because of the lost revenue resulting from this boycott, another shareholder of Company R believes that it may be possible to succeed in a shareholder's derivative suit alleging a waste of corporate assets resulting from negligent and/or unlawful activity by the officers and directors; an injunction and possibly a monetary recovery by the company (from the officers and directors) might be the result. The shareholder, however, has far fewer than the minimum number of shares a plaintiff must own to avoid the state statutory requirement of posting a bond at the commencement of such litigation. Because the bond would be prohibitively expensive, and because the addition of the university's shares would obviate such a bond, the shareholder asks the university to join him as a plaintiff.

After lengthy consideration of the merits of the case and interviews with company representatives, the council concludes that the company has failed to take adequate steps to house its migrant workers and that state and federal laws can not cope with this situation. Accordingly, the council recommends that the university agree to join the other shareholder as a plaintiff. The trustees accept this recommendation (by a divided vote), and the suit is commenced.

Approximately one month later, however, the university's portfolio managers conclude that the boycott is so severe that it may soon affect the price of the stock. The managers ask the treasurer if there is any objection to a sale of the stock. The treasurer consults the council, and it is agreed that the Guidelines do not prevent the sale from taking place; paragraph B1(a) states that "[m]aximum economic return will be the exclusive criterion for selection and retention" of securities (except in situations not applicable here). Accordingly, the sale is permitted to take place, even though it means that the university has to drop out as plaintiff, and the remaining plaintiff will have to look for another substantial partner.

CASE S

An individual shareholder of Company S, which operates a chain of supermarkets, writes to the university—also a shareholder of Company S—asking the university to join with him in a letter to management protesting the sale of any foodstuffs which result from animal slaughter. "Man no longer needs to be a predator to survive or stay healthy," the shareholder writes, "and therefore the slaughter of other living beings can no longer be justified; we will have to find ways of amusing our palates which do not involve killing."

One member of the council asks that the request be rejected as "frivolous." A majority of the council, however, believes that the letter poses a substantial moral issue; the members are reinforced in this belief by a memo from the director of University Dining Halls reporting a sharp increase in the number of students requesting vegetarian menus.

The council notes that the Guidelines state that social injury means "the injurious impact which the activities of a company are found to have on consumers, employees, or other persons. . . ." Although *social injury* does not therefore appear to refer to animals, the council considers whether or not it should act under paragraph B2(d), authorizing (but not requiring) a vote on proposals related to social questions but *not* involving social injury. Passing the question of whether a letter to management (i.e., something other than a vote) could be authorized by this provision, the council concludes that, in any event, it could not act on the shareholder's suggestion; despite the report from the director of Dining Halls, the cause of vegetarianism does not appear to have sufficiently widespread support within the university community. The council so informs the shareholder.

5. Legal Aspects of Investment Responsibility

INTRODUCTION

The discussion in the preceding chapters—and the Guidelines we have proposed—raise legal questions in three areas:

1. The corporation: whether, and in what manner, the officers or directors of a business corporation, with anything less than unanimous shareholder approval, can expend corporate funds or forego corporate profits in an effort to reduce the social injury caused by the company.
2. The shareholder: whether, and in what manner, the shareholders as a body can take formal action directing or requesting the officers and directors to take steps to reduce social injury.
3. The university-as-shareholder: whether, and in what manner, the university can exercise its shareholder rights to participate in shareholder action to reduce corporate social injury, or failing such an effort (and in a grave case), sell the securities involved.

The first two questions will be addressed by counsel for the corporations involved and counsel for protesting shareholders. It is only the third question that universities will have to resolve for themselves. Accordingly, in this introductory section we offer only a skeletal outline of a response to the first two questions, devoting most of the chapter to the question of the university's own legal capacity.

What Can Corporate Management Do?

The Expansive View. Almost thirty years ago E. Merrick Dodd, Jr., predicted that the law would soon permit social considerations to form the explicit basis for corporate activity:[1]

> [P]ublic opinion, which ultimately makes law, has made and is today making substantial strides in the direction of a view of

the business corporation as an economic institution which has a social-service as well as a profit-making function. . . . [T]his view has already had some effect upon legal theory, and . . . it is likely to have a greatly increased effect upon the latter in the near future. . . .

A sense of social responsibility toward employees, consumers, and the general public may thus come to be regarded as the appropriate attitude to be adopted by those who are engaged in business. . . .

Largely as a result of legislation in most states, it is fairly clear that Dodd's prediction has come true in relation to corporate charitable contributions.[2] But with respect to other aspects of socially related corporate conduct, the acceptance of his expansive view is far less certain. This view finds partial expression in the broad language of the leading case in the field, *A. P. Smith Mfg. Co. v. Barlow*, decided by the New Jersey Supreme Court:

More and more [corporations] have come to recognize that their salvation rests upon a sound economic and social environment. . . .It seems to us that just as the conditions prevailing when corporations were originally created required that they serve public as well as private interests, modern conditions require that corporations acknowledge and discharge social as well as private responsibilities as members of the communities within which they operate.[3]

But the case itself dealt only with charitable contributions; to our knowledge, the courts have not yet expressed similar sentiments when dealing with other kinds of socially oriented corporate activity.[4] Neither, on the other hand, have the courts forced the managers to "regard profit maximization as the goal of corporate existence."[5]

The reason the courts have managed to avoid taking a stand on either side of this question is that when management decisions have been challenged as excessively altruistic, the courts have justified these actions as serving the long-run business interests of the firm. This business-purpose rationale for the socially oriented activities of corporations is more constricted in theory than the approach discussed by Dodd—but the *results* are no less expansive.

The Business-Purpose View. Phillip I. Blumberg has summed up the rationales that the courts have used or will use to justify socially responsible corporate decisions:

Business efforts dealing with the community crisis may not only be reasonably related to the long-term profit-making potential of the corporation and its long-term ability to survive and prosper. They may also reflect the businessman's appraisal of the public acceptance-expectation-demand process and his decision as a business matter that it is "good business" to assume some responsibility for the community in which the corporation functions. In a public relations-oriented business world, the ramifications on the corporation's posture in its industry, on product acceptability, and its "image," on employee relations, on product acceptability, on investor reaction and on market performance of the shares seem reasonably clear. Even though the activity may have no immediate profit-orientation, it still may well represent a business-oriented decision to advance the long-term position and interests of the corporation, with the expenditure regarded as a politically inevitable cost of doing business.[6]

There are a number of precedents to support this view. For example, a federal district court used the business-judgment rule to approve (in *dicta*) a corporation's financing of its foreign operations by borrowing abroad (more expensively), a course of action apparently dictated in part by a desire not to aggravate the American balance-of-payments deficit.[7] Another company was permitted to give up profitable night-baseball games that the directors thought would contribute to deterioration of the neighborhood; an Illinois court justified this decision on the ground that it was in the long-run interest of the company to protect the value of the property on which its stadium sat.[8]

Under this business-purpose approach, corporate managers should have little trouble justifying activities—even costly activities—to reduce social injury in the name of long-run corporate viability. In so stating, however, we do not say that this needs to be (or is in fact) the motive for *university* efforts to correct such social injury. We only say that the *corporation* can and usually will defend its socially corrective conduct on this basis.[9] And in any case where the directors conclude that their activities are *unlawful* (e.g., under environmental or civil rights laws), they clearly have the power to correct the offending practices without bothering to establish a business justification; no such rationale is needed to bring a company into compliance with the law of the land.

What Can the Shareholder Do?

Under case law and statutes, the traditional rule of corporate governance is that "[t]he board of directors is the supreme authority in matters of management of the regular and ordinary business affairs. Their authority, however, does not extend to fundamental changes in organization, as to which shareholders are by statute given certain voting powers."[10]

Where does this leave the shareholders when they seek to correct corporate social injury? They are, of course, free to try to oust the directors in order to readjust the firm's social stance. And certain actions which may be deemed "fundamental changes in organization" will have social consequences—for example, charter amendments to prohibit manufacture of certain products or by-laws requiring that information relating to social injury be delivered to the shareholders.[11] It is unclear, however, how general policy directives (for example, a shareholder resolution that the corporation should increase antipollution activities or decrease production of antipersonnel weapons) would fare under the general rule quoted above. We believe that such policy directives would not violate the concept that shareholders are not to manage "regular and ordinary business affairs." But the case law here and in the entire area of shareholder power is surprisingly sparse.[12]

What fragments of precedent there are arise mainly under the SEC regulations determining which categories of shareholder proposals the management must include in its proxy materials. Because the use of the management proxy materials is the only economically feasible way for a shareholder to circulate and gain adherence for his proposals in a large public company, the SEC rules on this subject are of great importance. Under these rules, the management may omit shareholder proposals under three circumstances that are pertinent here:[13]

[1] If the proposal ... is, under the law of the [corporation's] domicile, not a proper subject for action by security holders; or

[2] If it clearly appears that the proposal is submitted by the security holder ... primarily for the purpose of promoting general economic, political, racial, religious, social or similar causes;[14] or

[3] If the proposal consists of a recommendation or request that the management take action with respect to a matter relating to the conduct of the ordinary business operations of the [corporation].

Does the language of these rules favor the inclusion of social-injury resolutions in management proxy materials? Such a resolution should meet the second test: it would not be introduced "primarily for the purpose of *promoting general ... social ... causes*" (emphasis supplied), but for the purpose of terminating a specific social harm caused by the company's own activities.[15] And such a resolution would not run afoul of the third test if it were not worded as a recommendation. Even if it were a recommendation, it would satisfy the third rule if, as we think likely, the correction of socially injurious activity does not constitute the "conduct of ... ordinary business operations"; i.e., the adjustment of the social policies of the company is not an example of an operational decision typically made on business grounds by corporate management. And if we are correct on this point, it also means that a social-injury resolution would not offend the first SEC test, for that test turns on the state law regulating the powers of shareholders; and under state law, the only prohibition on shareholder action (or at least the only *clear* area of prohibition) relates to shareholder attempts to run the "ordinary and regular business" of the company.

Definitive interpretations of the SEC rules, however, are not yet available. Just as the state courts have been generally uninformaative on the scope of shareholder powers, so have the federal courts been fairly silent on the interpretation of the SEC's rules governing shareholder proposals. Prior to 1970, only one court case considered the second of these rules ("economic, political . . . causes").[16] And prior to 1970, none of the judicial precedents developed under the first and third of these provisions related to shareholder proposals dealing with the kind of social injury questions we have been discussing.[17] In July 1970, the first appellate court decision dealing directly with the applicability of any of these three rules to social-injury proposals was handed down. In *Medical Committee for Human Rights* v. *SEC*,[18] the Court of Appeals for the District of Columbia reviewed the Dow Chemical Company's refusal to include a shareholder proposal asking the directors to consider amending the charter to prohibit napalm manufacture. (Dow invoked the second and third of the rules; the charter amendment approach was probably the reason the company did not rely on the first of these rules, relating to proper subject for shareholder action.) The SEC had supported Dow's refusal. The court dealt principally with judicial review questions in its opinion and did not reach a final decision on the merits of the commission's action. Yet, in remanding the case to the SEC for further explanation of its ruling, the court strongly suggested its disagreement with the commission. The court wrote:

As our earlier discussion indicates, the clear import of the language, legislative history, and record of administration of section 14(a) is that its overriding purpose is to assure to corporate shareholders the ability to exercise their right—some would say their duty—to control the important decisions which affect them in their capacity as stockholders and owners of the corporation. . . . No reason has been advanced in the present proceedings which leads to the conclusion that management may properly place obstacles in the path of shareholders who wish to present to their co-owners, in accord with applicable state law, the question of whether they wish to have their assets used in a manner which they believe to be more socially responsible but possibly less profitable than that which is dictated by present company policy.[19]

The SEC has sought review of the judicial-review aspects of this decision. If the decision is not disturbed by the Supreme Court and if the Court of Appeals, after hearing further from the SEC, proceeds to reaffirm the views it expressed in the initial decision, shareholders should be able to place many or most social-injury questions before their fellow owners at corporate meetings.[20]

We are brought, then, to the question of what role a university —operating within its own legal framework—may play in these corporate controversies.

THE UNIVERSITY AS RESPONSIBLE INVESTOR

A Summary of the Legal Objections

Governmental regulation of nonprofit colleges and universities is based on two main sources of legal authority: the power of state courts to regulate the fiduciary behavior of the trustees of charitable trusts or the directors of charitable corporations,* and the power of the federal and state taxing authorities to enforce the conditions upon which a school enjoys federal income tax exemption (and the benefit of receiving deductible contributions) and exemption from state and local property taxes. When the governing body of a university is asked to take social or moral considerations into account in making investment management decisions, the legal objections draw upon both of these sources of authority and may be summarized as follows:

First, the prudent-man rule, applicable under state law to trustees of private and charitable trusts and usually to directors of charitable corporations as well, is violated when trustees do not

---

*Universities (and other charitable entities) are organized either as charitable corporations or as charitable trusts. Frequently in this chapter, as elsewhere in this book, we have followed the common practice of using the word trustee to refer not only to trustees of a trust but also to the directors (or fellows or managers) of a charitable corporation.

invest with exclusive concern for maximizing economic return and capital safety (and perhaps capital growth as well).[21]

Second, where the social or moral interests are not those that the charitable corporation or trust is organized to serve, the directors will violate the corporate charter (or trust instrument) if they seek to promote these interests and, in so doing, they may also violate the terms of federal or state tax exemption conditioned on compliance with the charter or instrument.

Third, the university's donors intended their gifts to be used in accordance with the terms of its corporate charter or trust instrument, and any use of donated property to advance other interests therefore violates the conditions of gift. A narrower version of this contention arises where these other social or moral interests *are* embraced by the trust instrument or corporate charter but exceed the terms of a particular special-purpose gift—and where it is the property transmitted by that gift (or successor property) that is involved in the disputed investment.[22]

Fourth, the pursuit of social or moral causes is "political," or at least noneducational, in nature and therefore violates the conditions of federal income tax exemption and possibly state property tax exemption as well.

Although the last of these objections, as we shall see, rests on a misconception of the tax statutes, the first three objections invoke well-established principles of the law of charity.[23] Adherence to these provisions, moreover, is enforcible in a state court of equity jurisdiction at the instance of the state attorney general. (Violations of the tax statutes are enforcible by federal or state taxing authorities.) That an established and enforcible legal standard exists, however, does not mean that it has been violated. Here, as elsewhere in the law, the question of violation must be resolved on the basis of specific facts, particularly since "social responsibility" can embrace a wide spectrum of investment activities with varying legal consequences.

We shall focus, then, on the legality of the specific approach we have outlined in the prior chapters and in the Guidelines,[24] beginning with the first three objections, all of which invoke the rules of conduct governing charitable fiduciaries.

The Prudent-Man, Charter-Violation, and Breach-of-Gift
Objections

In discussing objections alleging violation of the prudent-man investment rule, of charter purposes, and of the conditions of general-purpose and special-purpose gifts, we note that there are fifty
states' courts involved in policing trustees; there are hundreds of
colleges and universities with differing charters; and there have
been millions of general and special purpose gifts to these schools.
We have not attempted to conduct research on all fifty states—
nor, of course, on all the charters and gift instruments. At least
with respect to state law, however, we have sought to ascertain
generally prevailing principles and apply them to our proposed
Guidelines. We believe, too, that what we say about charters and
gifts will hold true for the vast majority of them. The possibility
of a different result in a particular state—or in the light of idiosyncratic charter or gift provisions—should be borne in mind by
the prudent reader.

We start by considering two legal rationales for our suggested
investment policy, which assume, respectively, that the policy
will maximize the return from the university's portfolio or will at
least result in no cost to the university. Neither rationale appears
to be a total justification for the policy as a whole, but they will
support the policy in many of its applications.

The Maximum-Return Rationale. It may be contended that the
investment policy we have outlined is legally justifiable as a sophisticated attempt to maximize the university's economic return
from its endowment and therefore need not be defended—and
cannot be attacked—as a social pursuit. In other words, if a company's correction of social injury can be justified under the business purpose test (as serving the long-term economic interests of
the corporation), the shareholding university can justify, on similar economic grounds, its efforts to bring about such correction.
Dartmouth's treasurer, John Meck, has stated that "often, what is
good socially is good from an investment standpoint. The most
enlightened companies are frequently in the forefront as investments."[25] And Harvard's treasurer, George Bennett, has said: "I

don't want to imply that I'm not a hardboiled seeker of profits ... but the avenue to reach that end has to be through good management, and companies won't long survive if they disregard the public interest."[26] Similar contentions were heard in the 1970 General Motors corporate responsibility controversy, where some of management's opponents argued that the proposed resolutions on pollution and race relations served the economic interests of the company as well as social interests. The long-run profitability of General Motors, it was said, was a function of its ability to lead the way in developing a clean car and also a function of its ability to attract minority-group customers by increasing its very low proportion of minority-group franchise-holders.

The legal strength of this maximum-return rationale is limited, however. In the first place, it is difficult to rely on this rationale where the fiduciaries do not (and could not honestly) contend that profitability was their major concern in adopting a social-responsibility investment policy—in other words, where an improved return is only a by-product of an investment policy adopted for social-moral reasons. To rely on economic return as the justification for a socially oriented investment decision, the economic-return rationale must be an independent and plausible motive for that investment decision. In some instances, to be sure, maximization of return can serve as such an alternative, independent basis for a university decision to seek correction of socially injurious corporate conduct. And if the trustees recite this alternative rationale as grounds for a particular decision, this recital alone will probably serve as legal justification for that particular decision. But this is not the same as a maximum-return explanation of an entire program, a comprehensive policy such as the one reflected in our Guidelines. We doubt that many boards of trustees would be willing to assert that they had adopted such a program solely or mainly in order to improve the portfolio return.

Timing presents another factor limiting reliance on an economic-return rationale. This rationale cannot be used unless there is some correspondence between the amount of time it will predictably take for the investment return to be affected by correcting (or failing to correct) the socially injurious corporate conduct and the amount of time the security in question would normally be held. Thus, where charitable fiduciaries vote their stock in favor of altered company policies that will probably result in larger profits in five years—but where these fiduciaries rarely hold any securities more than *two* years—it is hard to defend such a vote on maximum-return grounds (unless it is believed that, within two years, the anticipation of later earnings will be reflected in increased stock market values). Obversely, if it is clear that the company will not correct certain morally objectionable policies, and one probable result will be reduction in the company's profitability in about ten years, a sale of the securities by the fiduciary cannot rationally be based on this fiscal prediction if such securities are rarely held more than two years (unless the market, within that two-year period, can be expected to discount for later losses).

Some investment managers contend that, in initial contemplation, *all* investments are meant to be long-term, even though most of them do not end up that way. If this were true, it would answer the objection based on timing. We suspect, however, that empirical data, if it were available, would not sustain this long-term characterization of the time frame in which the modern, total-return-oriented portfolio manager operates. The investor's time-frame, it should be noted, may be much shorter than that of the corporation itself; as we noted at the start of this chapter, corporate managers may justify most social-responsibility decisions as necessary to long-term profitability or survival. In other words, it may be easier for the manager than for the investor to defend—on economic-return grounds—a particular self-regulatory activity.

Although social self-regulation may not advance a single company's earnings within an investor's limited time-frame, economic benefits may be realized—within the same period of time—by the industry as a whole or by the entire corporate sector, as Henry C. Wallich and John J. McGowan point out. And these same authors observe that this result will improve the return for the owner of a widely diversified portfolio of securities—such as a university. But this point does not necessarily provide a maximum-return justification for all social injury corrections, because Wallich and McGowan also note that the benefits of some corporate social policies will not be recaptured by the industry as a whole or by the corporate sector and thus will not be recaptured by corporate shareholders (except indirectly in their capacities as members of the larger society).[27]

There is a second version of the maximum-return justification for social investment decisions. Here, the point is not that profitability follows morality, but that a company's lack of morality may cause other institutions to sell large amounts of the company's stock, thus depressing market values—and therefore justifying, on economic grounds, a university's attempt to correct the company's moral stance before the selling deluge.

The only data we have, however, indicates that it would take a vastly greater deluge than any we can contemplate to make a sustained impact on market prices. The work of our seminar's economics team showed that even the largest sales in stock market history have not had a depressant effect. On individual days in 1962, 1964, and 1965, DuPont sold roughly 1.5 million, 4 million, and 3 million shares of General Motors stock pursuant to court order—each sale disposing of more than the total number GM shares held in 1968 by fifty of the largest colleges and universities.[28] Yet none of the sales depressed the stock for more than a day, and the price in fact rose steadily on two of these occasions. In 1965, the Ford Foundation sold six million shares of Ford Motor Company stock through underwriters—roughly 5 per cent of the outstanding shares (and probably well in excess of the holdings of all universities)—without more than a few hours' dip in market price.

In sum, the maximum-return rationale will support some or many, but not all, social investment decisions; moreover, trustees who are not able to assert that such a rationale was what moved them to adopt the policy we have proposed will find it difficult to employ this rationale as a legal justification.

The No-Cost Rationale. A partial justification of the proposed investment policy follows from one important feature of the recommended Guidelines. Under these Guidelines, the yield-and-safety strictures of the prudent-man investment rule are rarely disturbed, for all security selections and almost all retention decisions are to be based solely on economic considerations; indeed, where the exercise of shareholder rights significantly threatens the return, the securities are to be sold. We cannot say, however, that this no-cost feature serves as a complete legal defense, for success in correcting social injury might result in a modest reduction in return—not enough to cause the portfolio managers to sell the stock but perhaps not insignificant for legal purposes.* Moreover, even a total avoidance of any economic loss would not answer the objections grounded on violation of charter purposes or violation of conditions of gift.

It must be admitted that where the socially oriented investment action is virtually costless, as compared to one that is costly, the legal objection is a good deal less trenchant, or, at least much less likely to be pursued by a state attorney general or other potential plaintiff. Yet trustees will probably wish to avoid *any* violation of fiduciary obligation, even one which imposes no expense, and therefore we must continue the analysis.

Aside from the maximum-return and no-cost rationales, there are three legal justifications for our investment approach, which appear to meet all three of the legal objections under discussion. One rationale invokes the normal range of administrative discretion possessed by charitable trustees—especially the directors of charitable corporations. A second justification invokes the power or duty shared by the directors of all charitable trusts and corporations to avoid taking action which is illegal in the trust-law sense, i.e., involving a violation of law or public policy. The third rationale invokes the right and duty of the directors of an educational corporation to take action to promote a climate in which the educational process can flourish. In the succeeding sections of this chapter, we discuss each of these justifications in turn.

---

*But see note 34 on p. 193, quoting Burton G. Malkiel and Richard E. Quandt on the unlikelihood of loss in return from the voting of proxies on socially oriented proposals.

The Discretionary Powers Rationale. One way of approaching the issue of legality begins with this question: Does the program we have proposed in this study—not aiming at more than self-regulation of the university's participation in social injury, not calling for action beyond the exercise of a stockholder's legal rights, and mandating (with limited exceptions) the continuation of maximum-return portfolio policies—appear to fall within the normal range of administrative discretion of university trustees?

Most universities are organized as charitable corporations, rather than as trusts. And the directors of such charitable corporations enjoy a somewhat greater degree of discretionary authority than the trustees of charitable trusts.[29] But even the trustees of a charitable trust "have such powers as . . . are necessary or appropriate to carry out the purposes of the trust and are not forbidden by the terms of the trust."[30] Charitable trustees are allowed considerable latitude in making expenditure decisions, as illustrated by an Ohio case in which trustees for educational purposes were permitted to use their funds to supplement the income of faculty members enlisted in the Army. The court stated that it "will not control [the] discretionary application of the funds [by charitable trustees] except to prevent abuse and misuse."[31]

Specifically with respect to the voting of proxies, Austin W. Scott, in his leading treatise on the subject, has stated:

> Where shares of stock are held in trust, the trustee may attend meetings of the shareholders and vote at such meetings as holder of the shares. In voting the shares he is under a duty to vote in such a way as to promote the interest of the beneficiaries. The trustee has discretion whether and how to vote, and if he does not abuse his discretion, the court will not interfere. Where he votes or threatens to vote in a manner which would be an abuse of the discretion and in violation of his duty to the beneficiaries, however, the beneficiaries can maintain a suit to prevent or redress the breach of trust.[32]

As mentioned earlier, most colleges and universities are organized as charitable corporations. Where investment questions are involved, the freedom of action of charitable corporation directors is noteworthy. On the basis of a recent study of the law relating to charitable endowments, Cary and Bright concluded:

> The law governing charitable corporations is not merely a branch of trust law, or corporate law, or contract law, but instead is sui generis, drawing to some extent on all three. Where the issue involves the investment of funds . . . the courts show a marked tendency to apply corporate principles rather than trust principles, in order to accord charitable corporations a maximum degree of flexibility.[33]

Another commentary states that "in those relationships and activities common to all corporations [charitable and noncharitable] the rights and liabilities of charities seem to be governed by the law pertaining to business corporations rather than that of trusts."[34]

Similarly, the Attorney General of New York has stated:

> Unless modified by statute, charter or by-laws, the powers of the trustees of an educational, religious or charitable corporation in respect to the administration and investment of the corporation's funds are fundamentally no different than that of the directors of a business corporation in respect to the administration of the property held by the corporation. . . .[35]

And in Connecticut, section 33-499 of the Connecticut General Statutes provides that the provisions of general corporate law shall apply to specially chartered corporations (including several colleges and universities).[36]

Accordingly, directors of charitable corporations have discretion that approaches, if it does not reach, the latitude enjoyed by business corporation directors. The law governing the discretionary power granted to such directors has.been summarized as follows:

> In the absence of express restrictions by charter or statute, the management of a corporation has authority to enter into all contracts or transactions which may reasonably be deemed incidental to its authorized business. . . .[37]

None of this precedent suggests that any charitable corporation may disregard or exceed charter purposes or the conditions of special-purpose gifts. What it does mean is that the directors of a charitable corporation (including a university in corporate form) have considerable leeway in determining the best way to administer the corporation in order to advance those charter purposes or special donative purposes, and this freedom particularly applies to investment decisions.

In view of its minimal approach, the policy we have proposed appears to fit rather easily within the broad range of discretionary powers held by university trustees—or at least the powers held by the directors of universities organized in corporate form.

We believe that the foregoing, rather broad-brush rationale reflects the spirit in which most lawyers (including most state attorneys general and most judges) will appraise our suggested Guidelines. Nevertheless, we shall also set forth two additional justifications—the "illegality" rationale and the "educational-climate" rationale—which are addressed to the specific purposes and policies of the proposed Guidelines.

The Illegality Rationale. An important principle of the law of charity is stated as follows in Scott on *Trusts:*

> A charitable trust cannot be created for a purpose which is illegal. The purpose is illegal if the trust property is to be used for an object which is in violation of the criminal law, or if the trust tends to induce the commission of crime, or if the accomplishment of the purpose is otherwise against public policy. Questions of public policy are not fixed or unchanging, but vary from time to time and place to place. A trust fails for illegality if the accomplishment of the purpose of the trust is regarded as against public policy in the community in which the trust is created and at the time when it is created.[38]

This rule of illegality applies to charitable corporations as well as charitable trusts.[39] Because the cases that develop this and related rules arise under trust law, we shall analyze the rule in the trust context and then relate it to directors of charitable corporations.

As recited above in its usual form, this rule applies to illegality in the substantive programs of a charitable organization, rather than in the management functions; moreover, the rule refers to the illegality of provisions of the trust instrument rather than illegality in the conduct of trust business. But in neither of these respects is the rule so limited.

This proscription logically cannot be applied to substantive programs without also applying it to management activities (such as investment, purchasing, etc.) carried on as part of the overall operation of the charitable organization. The point of the rule is that charity—which receives various legal advantages on the assumption that it confers a public benefit[40]—should not continue to enjoy these preferences if it operates in defiance of law or public policy and therefore generates public injury rather than benefit. Such injury can result from the managerial functions of a charitable entity as well as its philanthropic functions. Thus, if a charitable trust instrument directed the trustees to obtain income by operating businesses that were unlawful in this country or abroad, the provision would be illegal within the meaning of the rule; if it could not be deleted under the doctrine of administrative deviation,[41] the trust itself would be invalid. The same result would be reached if an administrative provision of the charitable instrument called for action that was determined to be against public policy. The Connecticut Supreme Court of Errors so held even in the case of a private, *non*charitable trust; it struck out the donor's restrictions on the development of the real property in which the trust was invested—restrictions that "would carry a serious threat against the proper growth and development of the parts of the city [Waterbury] in which the lands in question are situated" and which therefore were "invalid as against public policy. . . ."[42] And the *Restatement of Trusts,* in a section dealing with the investment duties of all trustees, private and charitable, states: "In making investments . . . the trustee is not under a duty to the beneficiary . . . to comply with a term of a trust which is illegal. . . ."[43]

The "illegal" character of a trustee's action is not diminished by the fact that the action is discretionary and not compelled by the trust instrument. Thus, the Internal Revenue Service recently invoked the illegality rule in a case involving the administrative policies—rather than the charter provisions—of a charitable organization; it held that a private school, by failing to operate under a "racially nondiscriminatory policy as to students," contravened "Federal public policy" and therefore was not " 'charitable' within the common law concepts"—even though no charter provision mandated discrimination (Revenue Ruling 71-447).

As we have stated, the illegality rule applies to noncharitable as well as charitable trusts. Similarly the illegality rule—or its close cousin—applies to noncharitable, as well as charitable, corporation; thus, obedience to federal, state and local statutes is probably an inherent provision of the charter of every business corporation. But in the case of a *charitable* entity it is even clearer that lawfulness and nonviolation of public policy are essential and, indeed, defining attributes. Thus, Scott has written: "The courts may do much to curb the testator's whims in the case of charitable trusts which they cannot do in the case of strictly private trusts."[44]

The judges of the state equity courts and the state attorneys general are not the only persons who can police what the *Restatement of Trusts* refers to as illegality (violation of criminal law or public policy) in the operation of a charitable trust or corporation. The trustees themselves have this same authority, as suggested by the *Restatement* language concerning the investment duties of all trustees, charitable and noncharitable: "the trustee is not under a duty . . . to comply . . . with a term . . . which is illegal.[45] The point is made even clearer in §166, a section not confined to investment questions, which sets forth the general rule that the trustee need not comply with illegal provisions; the section is followed by an official comment stating: "If the trustee is in doubt whether a term of the trust is illegal, he may apply to the proper court for instructions."[46] Scott makes the point more explicitly:

Is the trustee justified in deviating from the terms of the trust without first obtaining the authorization of the court to do so?. . . Where the terms of the trust are illegal or otherwise against public policy he is . . . justified.[47]

Plainly, then, the trustee is not required to seek judicial instructions before acting to correct illegality.

The *Restatement* language quoted above speaks only of what the trustee is "not under a duty" to do. In several situations he is under a positive duty *not* to engage in illegal conduct; to quote § 166 of the *Restatement:*

(1) The trustee is not under a duty to the beneficiary to comply with a term of the trust which is illegal.

(2) The trustee is under a duty to the beneficiary not to comply with a term of the trust which he knows or should know is illegal, if such compliance would be a serious criminal offense or would be injurious to the interest of the beneficiary or would subject the interest of the beneficiary to an unreasonable risk of loss.[48]

In the quoted section, which applies to charitable and private trustees alike, the scope of the duty *not* to comply (paragraph (2)) is narrower than the power to avoid compliance (paragraph (1)); in particular, public-policy violations are not included in the duty *not* to comply unless such violations injure the beneficiary. Perhaps the reason for limiting the duty *not* to comply is that judgments as to illegality are often difficult to make, particularly where the illegality consists of a violation of public policy; the existence of a duty to avoid public policy violations (i.e., a duty *not* to comply) would require a trustee to make such difficult decisions at the peril of being found guilty of a breach of trust.

Indeed, the fact that public policy is an elusive concept means that there is some danger in pressing the notion that a trustee has a *duty* based on this doctrine, or, generally, in encouraging the courts to use this concept as a ground for policing the decisions of a charitable body. One of the great virtues of the charitable sector is that it can experiment with programs or policies that are not in favor with, or that are opposed by, majoritarian sentiment; in this pluralistic feature resides a supremely important reason for encouraging the birth and growth of philanthropic institutions. It is perhaps for this reason that, while the doctrine of invalidation of charitable trust provisions for violation of public policy is still good law, it has been applied in few reported clases. For the same reasons, it seems likely that the category of public-policy violation most likely to be the object of state intervention will be conduct that frustrates the ability of public agencies to enforce legal norms. If courts and attorneys general enforced only this category of public-policy violation—where there is a fairly objective external guide to intervention—the danger of state control of charitable programs would significantly recede. In fact, our suggested Guidelines single out this category of public-policy violation for special emphasis. (See the definition of *social injury*, paragraph A2(e).)

Yet this safeguard—tying the definition of *public policy* to external legal norms—is unnecessary where the policing of public-policy violations is carried out, not by the state, but by the trustees themselves. It is one thing to fear the impact of a broad-ranging public-policy doctrine as a ground for the government imposing its value preferences on the work of the voluntary sector. It is quite another thing, however, when this doctrine is invoked on the trustees' own motion to control charitable activity where its impact appears to violate what the trustees perceive to be public policy. In other words, there seems to be a sound reason for the *Restatement's* rule that the *power* of a trustee to avoid illegality is broader than his *duty* to do so.

When exercising his power to avoid illegality, can the trustee act upon a more expansive notion of what constitutes a violation of law or public policy than a court would have adopted? Perhaps not, if the trustee wishes to take the exceptional step of deviating from an explicit term of the trust. But where the trustee wishes only to manage his investments or exercise his shareholder powers to avoid illegality, and where he observes the ever-present duties of care and skill and caution in so acting, there is no reason to tie the trustee's judgment to a judicial perception of illegality. The cases we have examined do not impose such an obligation. (They do not deal with the question at all.) And there is ample factual precedent for the exercise of such discretion by both charitable and noncharitable trustees. Thus, it is often the case that trustees implement their po.. ers by invoking some notion of law or public policy that a court might not have endorsed—for example, when boards of charitable or noncharitable organizations implement the general prohibition against self-dealing by establishing stricter voting-disqualification rules than the courts would impose, or when trustees undertake pension obligations to employees on the basis of public-policy notions not yet expressed in law.[49]

These conclusions about the power of charitable trustees to manage their investments so as to avoid illegality (violations of law and of public policy) apply even more strongly to directors of educational and other charitable corporations. As already pointed out, the general proposition that charities may not serve illegal purposes applies to charitable corporations as well as trusts. More-over, the fact that charitable corporation directors are widely understood to have greater investment discretion than charitable trustees (see pp. 142-43) permits the assumption that the powers held by the trustee group respecting illegality must repose, in even greater abundance, with the directors of charitable corporations.

We must now consider two further questions in connection with the exercise of this power. The first question asks what we mean when we say that a charitable organization is involved in or par-ticipates in illegality; the second relates to the definition of *public policy*.

Turning to the first of these questions, critics of our approach might contend that it is farfetched for a charitable organization to contend that it is correcting *its own* illegal conduct when it seeks to modify the illegal conduct of a public corporation in which it holds a minute percentage of shares. (In the case of a university, share ownership rarely exceeds 1/10 of 1 per cent of outstanding stock and is usually much smaller.) In other words, the question is whether a university really participates in—is in-volved in—a violation of law or public policy committed by a major corporation, simply by owning shares and failing to chal-lenge the violation.[50] We do not mean participation or involve-ment in the sense of criminal or civil liability for the corporation's acts. The doctrine of limited liability—the cornerstone of corporation law—precludes such a result except where corporate status has been imperfectly achieved or grossly disregarded.[51] Instead, *participation* or *involvement* refers to a relationship to the corporate activity that could rationally support a feeling of responsibility for that activity on the part of a shareholder, quite apart from legal liability.

On a somewhat formalistic level, this question can be answered in terms of traditional corporate-law doctrine. While the law precludes the shareholder's day-to-day control of business affairs,[52] it nonetheless names the shareholder as an owner. In legal contemplation there are no owners other than the holders of equity shares. Surely an "owner" is "involved" in a transgression committed by "his" company. His "involvement," obviously, is fractional. But so, in one degree or another, is the involvement of all the other owners of the company, unless it is a one-man corporation. The corporate form is designed to permit dispersed ownership, and dispersed or fractional involvement in corporate activity is a necessary corollary. Accordingly, if involvement is ignored because it is fractional, that implies a rejection of the doctrine of corporate ownership. As long as this doctrine is respected, all owners must be regarded as having some form of involvement and participation in whatever social injury the corporation inflicts.

Somewhat similar reasoning appears in what is probably the first judicial decision even tentatively to touch upon the issue of shareholder authority to control corporate social responsibility. The D.C. Circuit Court of Appeals, after referring to the shareholders' "right—some would say their duty—to control the important decisions which affect them in their capacity as stockholders and owners of the corporation," suggested that one such important decision was "the question of whether they wish to have their assets used in a manner which they believe to be more socially responsible but possibly less profitable than that which is dictated by present company policy."[53]

The ownership concept, however, is not in favor among many modern legal commentators, who find that corporate law does not accord much respect to the ownership status of shareholders and who urge that we understand the relations between share-holder and company in terms of function rather than title.[54] A functional analysis of the participation question, however, leads to the very same conclusion.

In the first place, an institutional shareholder who votes routine-ly for management and who otherwise fails to complain about corporate practices lends a measure of apparent acceptance and approval to existing corporate policies, thus reinforcing the man-agement's predisposition to pursue these policies. In other words, until a shareholder ends his acquiescence in corporate violations of law or public policy, he encourages their continuation.

A shareholder may be considered to participate in his com-pany's misconduct in a second sense. It seems fair to say that a person participates in a wrong if he has the power to end it and fails to use that power. The shareholders of a corporation have the power to end corporate violations of law or public policy, despite the difficulty of using that power collectively. Although the question of whether the shareholders may direct the existing directors to alter corporate practices has not been authoritatively resolved,[55] the shareholders may replace the directors with other directors who will behave differently. With the cooperation of these directors—or, in some states, without it—the shareholders can amend the charter to alter corporate policy.[56] In the last analysis, then, the final responsibility rests with the shareholders. By failing to exercise their last-resort authority within the corpo-rate structure, they participate in the continuation of a violation. And when an individual shareholder fails to do what he or she (or it) can reasonably do to bring about such collective shareholder action, that shareholder, individually, participates in the continu-ation of the violation. The Guidelines we are considering require a university to do no more than to terminate such participation.

The second question raised in connection with self-policing power relates to the definition of *public policy*. In some situa-tions, a corporate practice perceived as a social harm by a uni-versity-shareholder may not be perceived that way by many or most members of the general public. In such a case, how can the practice be viewed as a violation of public policy so as to fall within the illegality doctrine we are analyzing?

The question presents no difficulty where the company practice, although not itself a violation of law, frustrates the enforcement of some norm of domestic or international law. Here, notwithstanding public attitudes, the conduct is inconsistent with a policy that has become a part of the law enacted or enunciated by a public body—a legislative body (or an administrative agency carrying out legislation) or a court. To these bodies the general public has given over its authority to act; these bodies make or declare what can fairly be called public policy. Most of the shareholder actions that might be taken pursuant to our recommended approach would meet this criterion of public policy. The university will usually be reacting to corporate activities that (in the language of the proposed Guidelines) "violate, or frustrate the enforcement of, rules of domestic or international law"—either by voting or speaking out against such conduct or by supporting new corporate procedures or new personnel likely to prevent such conduct.

Where there is no established legal norm that has been violated or frustrated, a university or other charitable organization is nevertheless entitled to conclude that a corporate practice violates public policy because of the social injury it inflicts, even though this judgment may not be shared by a majority of the general public. Scott implies a majoritarian approach when he states that "a trust fails for illegality if the accomplishment of the purposes of the trust is regarded as against public policy in the community in which the trust is created and at the time when it is created."[57] But the criterion to be used for judicial intervention to strike down the trust itself, *ab initio,* is not necessarily the same criterion that should be used when the trustees are regulating their own activities. As we have already indicated, judicial policing of public policy violations presents the danger of official intrusion into the content of charitable programs; the danger, obviously, is aggravated if the court reflects only its own biases. For this reason (and possibly for reasons related to the role of the courts in our governmental system),[58] if there is to be any judicial intervention—particularly where it results in the invalidation of the entire trust—perhaps it should take place only in accordance with legislative norms or the majority opinion of some relevant "community." But we do not need to resolve this question here, for as we have seen, the perils of judicial intervention on public policy grounds do not apply where illegality is policed by charitable fiduciaries themselves. Accordingly, the protective reason for requiring majority support of a *court decision* based on public policy grounds does not pertain to *self-policing* based on such grounds.

Nor is such a majoritarian notion inherent in the expression *against public policy*. There is no semantic reason to suppose that it means any more than "against policies which are in the public interest." Indeed, that is all the expression seems to mean in the one other area of trust law in which it appears—the provisions of *private* trust law that define "a large and miscellaneous class of trusts which are held invalid on the ground that their enforcement would be against public policy."[59] Although Scott states, in connection with these provisions, that "questions of public policy depend on conceptions which are prevalent in the community at the time when the transaction takes place,"[60] the case law does not seem to reflect any judicial effort to count heads in the community. For example, the cases holding that private trust provisions are invalid because they serve "capricious purposes" (e.g., to cause a house to be bricked up for twenty years or to keep a clock in repair), or because they relieve a trustee from any liability for bad-faith breaches of trust, seem to be bottomed not on an assessment of majority opinion but on a judicial conception of the public interest.[61] For that matter, the most celebrated trust-law prohibition based on public policy—the rule against perpetuities—originated with judicial determinations of the social and economic need to achieve "two chief objectives . . . [:]to curtail dead-hand domination and facilitate marketability."[62] The English and later American courts that developed the rule do not appear to have asked whether a majority of the people agreed with these determinations. Once again we pass over the libertarian and jurisprudential implications of this bit of legal history, which we recite solely to point out that *public policy* has not traditionally incorporated a majoritarian criterion.

Accordingly, we do not believe that charitable fiduciaries are deprived of discretion to avoid a violation of public policy simply because their judgment, if a public poll were taken, might turn out to be a minority opinion. If, for example, the fiduciaries believed that it was against public policy for a company in which they hold stock to refuse to hire women (before the Civil Rights Act of 1964) or to continue to manufacture nerve gas, their investment action based on this belief would not become unlawful because a poll demonstrated that most citizens did not subscribe to sex equality or did not object to the production of nerve gas.

Limits of reasonableness obtain here as elsewhere. An impulsive decision not based on analysis of the public interest—a decision without *any* substantial support in the community and reflecting little more than private predilection—would represent an abuse of discretion. Reasonableness has its quantitative as well as qualitative aspects. It would be difficult, on the basis of the illegality doctrine, for a trustee to justify rejecting almost all likely investment opportunities or devoting much of the charity's income to corporate proxy fights.[63] But where the charitable organization acts carefully and selectively in an effort to prevent companies of which it is a shareholder from violating law or public policy, the law of charity will give its approval.

Returning to the three categories of legal objection set forth earlier—objections based on the prudent-man rule, on the duty to obey the corporate charter, and on the duty to honor gift conditions—let us consider each in the light of the illegality rationale.

First, the prudent-man rule must coexist with other rules, including those pertaining to the power of a trustee to avoid illegality. Accordingly, the prudent-man rule can demand maximization of return only up to the point it is consistent with the fiduciary's exercise of his coexisting power relating to avoidance of illegality. The trustee who properly and reasonably exercises his power to avoid violation of law or public policy cannot simultaneously be accused of imprudence because of a failure to maximize investment return, any more than a trustee who properly exercises his power to compromise or abandon a claim on behalf of the trust estate can be accused of failing thereby to honor his duty to preserve trust property.[64] Indeed, the formulation of the prudent-man rule in the *Restatement of Trusts* explicitly acknowledges that a trustee is not under a duty to comply with a trust provision that is illegal in the sense in which we have been using it.[65]

Second, a charity's trust instrument or corporate charter—unless it expressly states otherwise—necessarily incorporates the fiduciary power we have described here, just as it incorporates all of the rest of the law of charity. Accordingly, the proper exercise of power to avoid illegality cannot violate the charter or trust instrument.

Third, in the absence of clear instructions to the contrary, it must be assumed that any donor to a charitable organization, whether his gift is for general support or for special purposes, contributes with the understanding that his contribution will be administered in accordance with the rules of law governing charitable fiduciaries. Thus, the conditions of a general or special purpose gift are not violated when the trustees make investment decisions with respect to the donated property in a manner designed to discharge their power to avoid illegality—unless the language of the gift specifically precludes such investment decisions (we have not yet seen an example of such language).

The doctrine we have set forth is a conservative and narrowly focused doctrine. Once in a while, a court has permitted trustees to take a much more aggressive stance with respect to the inclusion of moral or social criteria in investment decisions. A notable example, particularly because it involves a *non*charitable trustee, is a decision by the Surrogate's Court of New York County, affirmed by the Appellate Division, which permitted the trustee to invest, during World War I, in 3½ per cent First Liberty Loan Bonds despite a specific instruction by the testator to invest in 4 per cent railroad bonds. The Surrogate wrote:

> These are abnormal times. Our country is engaged in a great war and needs the undivided support, aid and loyalty of every citizen. Under these circumstances the court should not be bound

by narrow and restricted rules of law and construction in questions which affect the welfare of our country, but should exercise its best and wisest discretion. The investment by the trustees in Liberty Loan bonds was in aid of our government in its hour of need, and they should be commended rather than condemned therefor.[66]

Scott regards this as an aberrational result that most courts would reject.[67] By contrast, the approach we have outlined—which seeks no more than the avoidance of "illegality" (violation of law or public policy)—rests securely within the mainstream of the law of charity.

The illegality rationale we have set forth may be briefly summed up in nontechnical language: The trustees of a charitable body are not required to engage in or support activities which the trustees reasonably believe to contravene the public interest, and they may exercise their shareholder rights to deter a corporate management from undertaking such activities for their account.

The Educational-Climate Rationale. We turn now to another legal justification for the investment management Guidelines we have suggested, a rationale consistent with but independent of the avoidance-of-illegality rationale. The alternative justification focuses on the power of the trustees of a university to make administrative decisions that will help to foster a climate conducive to education.

We have already discussed the considerable latitude to make administrative decisions that is enjoyed by the trustees of charitable trusts. The managerial authority vested in the directors of educational and other charitable corporations is even broader, as we have also noted; it approaches the discretionary powers held by directors of business corporations. One example of the customary freedom of action enjoyed by business directors involves the expenditure of funds to improve interpersonal relations within the company. Lord Justice Bowen expressed the principle this way in a nineteenth century English case:

The law does not say that there are to be no cakes and ale, but there are to be no cakes and ale except such as are required for the benefit of the company. . . . The Master of the Rolls . . . held that the company might lawfully expend a week's wages as gratuities for their servants: because that sort of liberal dealing with servants eases the friction between masters and servants, and is, in the end, a benefit to the company.[68]

One problem universally faced by universities today, to use Bowen's language, is to "ease the friction" between and among the components of the university community—students, administration, faculty, and alumni. It is a friction that erupts into violent confrontation from time to time and in any case heats up the climate of academic life to a point which impedes the ability of students and faculty to work effectively—or so a university board of trustees might reasonably conclude on the basis of personal observation.

By all accounts, one crucial factor contributing to this friction is a weakening of the fabric of trust and confidence among members of the university population—particularly trust on the part of the students as they look upon trustees, administrators, and faculty. That this breakdown largely coincides with, and may be partly caused by, generational differences makes the breakdown no less real and no less counterproductive. As McGeorge Bundy has written, "The integrity of the [university] community is at risk and . . . the maintenance of confidence among all members of the community is now the indispensable component of an effective attack upon the danger. . . ."[69] One important factor leading to the loss of such confidence—as university trustees might reasonably conclude from recent events—is the widespread student belief that those in command of universities are insufficiently sensitive to the moral quality of university decisions. In an Urban Institute survey of attitudes, the fifth-ranking cause of campus unrest cited by both students and faculty (out of a total of nineteen causes) was "hypocrisy."[70] The controversies relating to ROTC, to defense contracts and research, and to university ownership of slum housing furnish examples of these perceptions of hypocrisy that may also be shared by some alumni.[71] Even more directly to the point are the controversies over university investments in "immoral" or "irresponsible" enterprises (including the confrontations over investments in companies with South African connections and the debates over the voting of proxies in the recent General Motors contests).

It is not altogether clear whether student concern about hypocrisy is a cause or a symptom of the breakdown of trust. But whether an attempt to meet this concern is causal or symptomatic treatment, it is a course of conduct that university trustees may plausibly regard as important for the restoration of a trusting relationship within the university family. And such a course of conduct would logically include the consideration of moral and social criteria in exercising shareholder rights. At a recent conference of endowment managers, Professor Colyer Crum of the Harvard Business School had these remarks to make about the relationship between student confidence and investment policies:

> An institutional investment manager or endowment manager who chooses not to get involved at this point in time is going to have a tough row to hoe. I don't think the students are going to let him off the hook. . . .
>
> So not only are you going to have to vote yes or no . . . but I think increasingly you are going to have to vote against the managers. You are going to have to do some arm-twisting in the public interest if you ever expect to be able to speak and be listened to.
>
> The students would like to see some action; I don't feel that they believe they have seen very much so far. So you have to decide yes or no, and then you have to increasingly, over the coming months and years, build a record that will be plausible. In other words, I don't think that it is any more a viable possibility to follow the traditional argument that says, "I am a money manager and damn the public consequences."
>
> It may be very difficult to include the social dimension without squandering your endowment. I have no doubt that this complicates matters a great deal, but I am equally convinced that ignoring these questions is not an available alternative.[72]

In the light of the foregoing, a university board of trustees may reasonably conclude that action to avoid participation in socially harmful activities will help to restore or maintain a climate sufficiently free from friction to promote effective teaching and scholarship. Because the creation of such a climate is within the charter purposes of any university, the directors of a charitable corporation are free to exercise their broad discretion to make investment management decisions which promote that climate.

Even where such measures result in some sacrifice of return (which we think will rarely be the case under the Guidelines we suggest), the resulting "expenditure" is, in legal principle, no different from the decision of a business corporation to promote morale and incentives among its work force by providing cakes and ale—or, in modern terms, stock options, pension benefits, and trips to Florida. Nor is such an expenditure any different, in legal principle, from the decision of university trustees to increase faculty morale by improving fringe benefits, or to enhance student morale by modernizing the dormitories, air-conditioning the library, or subsidizing the school paper.

When university resources are thus used to improve the climate for education, it is also immaterial whether the trustees take action by means of the expenditure of income or by means of the management of investment assets (unless there are special charter or donative restrictions on such investment usage). The difference reflects only an administrative choice among various ways to carry out charter purposes. This understanding—that there is no legal difference between investment decisions and income distribution decisions when both advance charter purposes—appears to be widely shared and implemented by university trustees. Such an understanding must underlie a university's use of investment assets to provide below-market-rate mortgages for faculty members as a way of improving their satisfaction with university life. This understanding must also be the premise for university loans on favorable terms to neighboring private schools, in order to permit these schools to increase their student capacity and thereby expand the educational options available to faculty children. The same observation may be made about university loans to real estate development enterprises in the university city or town, loans that may not represent the first choice of the portfolio managers but are calculated to improve the physical environment in which the university operates.

As compared to these uses of investment assets to improve the climate for education, an effort to improve that same climate by demonstrating moral sensitivity in investment and shareholder decisions raises no additional legal questions, for this use of assets differs only in technique. It is precisely to accommodate changes in technique that the law, as we have seen, allows great flexibility in the administration of charitable corporations.

This discussion of the managerial benefits of moral sensitivity in investment activities does not reflect a view that trustees will or should concern themselves with investment responsibility questions solely to *épater les étudiants*. In fact, trustees who take up the burden of inquiring into social consequences probably do so for dual reasons: because it seems to be the right thing to do and also because it helps to reduce the friction. We do not at all disparage the former motive; indeed it, rather than the administrative rationale, is what has motivated us to propose the policies set forth in this book. Yet we have emphasized the administrative motive in this section because, for trustees who embrace this rationale, it forms an independent basis for the lawfulness of the investment approach we are recommending.

We now return to the three categories of legal objection outlined earlier to examine each of them in the light of the legal justification we have been discussing.

First, with respect to the prudent-man rule, we have already pointed out that our proposed Guidelines will rarely result in a reduction of return. Moreover, the rule regulates the trustee only in his *return-producing* function and not with respect to any *programmatic* function that he may be carrying on via the use of investment assets. For example, if one part of a university portfolio consists of loans to students and mortgage loans to faculty members and the other part consists of conventional income-producing securities, only the latter portion would be subject to the full return-and-safety rigors of the prudent-man rule, even though both portions of the portfolio are composed of investments. The *Internal Revenue Code* recognizes this same distinction when it provides that "program-related investments" are not subject to the new rule prohibiting a private foundation from making investments of a speculative or unproductive nature that "jeopardize the carrying out of exempt [charitable] purposes"; the point is that the program-related investment *itself* carries out the exempt purposes.[73]

There is no reason why the very same investment may not simultaneously serve both return-producing and program-related functions; indeed this is really the true description of the mortgage loan to the faculty member. Here the prudent man rule's investment criteria must coexist with the programmatic needs to be served; *both* functions must be accommodated. In other words, the security must be prudently selected and managed in terms of income and safety but in a manner consistent with program-related objectives. If these objectives require a 6 per cent ceiling on mortgage loans to faculty members at a time when mortgages can be sold at 7 per cent in the market, 6 per cent will suffice (although the 6 per cent loans should otherwise be prudently made). The same reasoning applies to our proposed Guidelines: they can be explained as an effort to manage university investments in a manner which simultaneously serves an income-producing goal and a program-related mission—the mission of improving the climate for education.

Another way of expressing the same point is to say that the prudent-man rule itself must make room for administrative necessity. The word *prudent* permits this interpretation; as defined in the *Oxford English Dictionary,* it means: "of persons (rarely of inferior animals): Sagacious in adapting means to ends; careful to follow the most politic and profitable course; having or exercising sound judgment in practical affairs; circumspect, discreet, worldly-wise."

The second possible objection to our investment Guidelines—an objection based on deviation from charter purposes—is fully answered by the rationale we have been discussing, for that rationale treats these Guidelines as a method by which the trustees seek to *implement* the charter mandate.

Third, with respect to the objection based on donative conditions: an unrestricted gift is made to further the general purposes of the university as described in the charter; accordingly, the terms of such a gift are not defeated when the donated property is invested pursuant to policies designed to *advance* the charter purposes. Indeed, this same observation applies to most special-purpose gifts to a university. Although such a gift selects a portion of the spectrum of university activities to be supported, it rarely, if ever, prescribes that the donated property should be managed in ways—or informed by considerations—other than those which apply to the rest of the university's investment assets, thus referring us for guidance to the principles that govern general-purpose gifts.

Three additional points should be made about this educational-climate rationale. For one thing, it does not depend on student or faculty participation in the making of the investment decisions (although we have in fact recommended student and faculty inclusion in an advisory council); the university can demonstrate its sensitivity to important moral and social questions without necessarily altering its governance patterns. Nor, in order to utilize this legal rationale, is it necessary that each investment decision with respect to social injury be made in response to widespread student demand or protest; the building of student confidence is an ongoing, gradual process in which trustees can properly engage without waiting for a crisis to develop over a particular investment. Finally, the development of an improved climate for learning may include efforts to maintain alumni support; it would, therefore, be consistent with the rationale we are discussing for trustees to take alumni reactions into account when making an investment decision or exercising shareholder rights. (The proposed Guidelines place three alumni on the advisory council and call on the council to take into account the views of all constituents, including alumni.)[74]

The application of the educational-climate rationale is, of course, subject to limits of reasonableness. University trustees would abuse the discretion vested in them if they rejected all income-producing possibilities simply in order to satisfy those students who believe that all income derived from business profits is per se immoral. They would similarly abuse their discretion if they developed an investment review process so cumbersome that it would preclude efficient portfolio management. But the policies and procedures we have outlined do not begin to approach these extremes. They call upon the trustees to act on the basis of social injury sparingly and carefully and with great respect for the necessity of economic return.

A variation on the rationale we have just discussed could provide an alternative justification for our proposed investment management Guidelines. A salubrious climate for education is not only a function of good interpersonal relations within the university; it is also a function of the peace and health of the larger society. A cataclysm of major dimensions—world war, violent racial upheaval, or the collapse of the ecosystem—would sooner or later impair or terminate the functioning of the university. Its trustees might well conclude that socially injurious corporate actions increase the possibility of these cataclysmic events and that correction of such social injury therefore tends to protect the climate for education.

In principle, this rationale is not different from the commonly accepted notion that a university can use its income or its investment assets to help save its immediate environs from physical or social deterioration and to minimize town-gown antagonisms. As compared to this local-protection approach, the broader anti-cataclysm rationale contemplates a threat to the university that is more remote, both in time and in terms of the university's own impact on the outcome. Yet in both cases, the university purports to act in the interest of its own ultimate security.[75]

Moreover, in both the short-term, locally oriented and the long-term, nationally—or globally—oriented versions of this security rationale, there is an analogy to the legal justifications employed to bless the social activities of business corporations. As mentioned at the beginning of this chapter, the law appears to permit corporations to justify their charitable contributions and other pro bono actions not only in terms of immediate public-relations and community-relations advantages (short-term), but also in terms of impact on the environment in which business must operate (long-term). We believe that an educational corporation possesses legal capacity, similar to that of a business corporation, to safeguard the future climate for its chartered mission. The exercise of shareholder rights to reduce socially injurious corporate conduct represents a modest and reasonable step in this direction.

The legal objections we have been considering—invoking the prudent-man rule, charter purposes, and gift conditions—all relate to the fiduciary obligations of university trustees. We now turn to the fourth category of objections, which invokes not fiduciary principles but the dictates of federal and state tax laws.

The Tax Law Objections

It might be contended that a charitable trustee's consideration of social or moral factors in investment decisions is a political act, or at least a noneducational activity, which violates the conditions of federal and state tax exemption (and associated deductibility rules).

The Political Objection. To our knowledge, no objection to social investment decisions has been based on the political prohibitions of federal or state tax laws. Yet in the spring of 1970, a similar objection was lodged against universities that arranged their academic calendars to permit campaigning for peace candidates and that conducted apparently official efforts to lobby for passage of Vietnam withdrawal legislation. In any controversy over a socially oriented investment policy, one might hear echoes of the 1970 politics vs. tax-exemption arguments.

If we look at the university actions taken in the spring of 1970, however, we see that they were of a very different legal character from the actions called for by our investment Guidelines. The 1970 activities—which related to election campaigning and lobbying—invited scrutiny under the two sections of the Internal Revenue Code that impose political prohibitions on universities and other charitable organizations. Section 501(c)(3) provides that

a. Such an organization may not "participate in, or intervene in . . . any political campaign on behalf of any candidate for public office," and

b. "[N]o substantial part of the activities" of such an organization may consist of "carrying on propaganda, or otherwise attempting to influence legislation. . . ."

In addition, the Federal Corrupt Practices Act makes it unlawful for "any corporation whatever . . . to make a contribution or expenditure in connection with any election" to federal office, including primaries and conventions (18 U.S.C. §610); most universities are in corporate form.

With one indirect and insubstantial exception,[76] none of the university actions contemplated by our Guidelines involve either political campaigning or lobbying; they therefore breach neither of the Internal Revenue Code restrictions set forth above or the Corrupt Practices Act. Herein lies the essential legal difference between the university political activities of 1970 and the investment policies we propose.

Of course, it might be asserted that any effort to affect the social stance of corporations in controversial areas—involving, for example, the treatment of minorities at home (case L, chapter 4) or in South Africa (case H), or the production of anticivilian personnel weapons (case B)—is political in some larger sense; i.e., that any action that tries, with however minimal an effort, to affect processes of social change is political. Accepting such a definition of political for the moment, it does not follow that this kind of activity violates either federal or state tax exemption statutes. Even general statements (such as Judge Learned Hand's) about the incompatability of charitable exemption status with "political agitation" have been uttered in the specific context of lobbying or campaign activities.[77] And the current Treasury regulations interpreting the exemption statute expressly declare:

The fact that an organization, in carrying out its primary purpose, advocates social or civic changes or presents opinion on controversial issues with the intention of molding public opinion or creating public sentiment to an acceptance of its views does not preclude such organization from qualifying under section 501(c)(3) so long as it is not an [organization engaged in legislative or electoral activities].[78]

With respect to state tax exemption, we are aware of no administrative or judicial decisions in any state that differ from the position of the Treasury Department as quoted above.

One further point about the Treasury regulations remains to be noted. For a brief period about twenty years ago, educational organizations—as a specific subcategory of groups exempt under §501(c)(3) of the Internal Revenue Code—were enjoined by Treasury regulations to avoid "controversy" in their educational programs. This position was reversed in 1956, when the following language was substituted:

The term "educational," as used in section 501(c)(3), relates to—

(a) The instruction or training of the individual for the purpose of improving or developing his capabilities; or

(b) The instruction of the public on subjects useful to the individual and beneficial to the community.

An organization may be educational even though it advocates a particular position or viewpoint so long as it presents a sufficiently full and fair exposition of the pertinent facts as to permit an individual or the public to form an independent opinion or conclusion. On the other hand, an organization is not educational if its principal function is the mere presentation of unsupported opinion.[79]

Does the next-to-last sentence mean that if a university "advocates a particular position or viewpoint" in a stockholder's meeting, corporate board room, or court, in an effort to correct corporate social injury, it must present "a . . . full and fair exposition of the pertinent facts"? Probably not, for this wording is apparently intended to apply to cases where the overall educational character of the organization is in doubt—particularly cases where it is unclear that the organization, in terms of its overall purpose, fits under the "instruction of the public" category. This reading is reinforced by the reference to the "principal function" of the organization in the last sentence. It does not seem likely, from the context, that the Regulation meant to require that an unquestionably educational body like a university must—in its *non*educational (investing) capacity—present a "full and fair exposition" so as to assist "an individual or the public" to reach conclusions. In case this interpretation should be in error, which we think improbable, a university would still be free to proceed under our proposed Guidelines but would have to accompany its actions with a detailed and factual explanation—perhaps a wise procedure in any event.

In summary, the Guidelines we have outlined do not offend against the political prohibitions of the federal tax laws or, as far as we can tell, of any state tax laws.

The Noneducational Objection. Although politics does not seem to present a problem under the federal or state tax laws, it might be contended that our Guidelines jeopardize a university's tax exemption because they call upon a school to do something other than educate whereas education is all a university's federal or state tax exemption permits it to do, or education is all a university's charter permits it to do—and a violation of a charter also violates a tax exemption based on that charter. We consider these points in turn.

Since most universities have never applied for an exemption ruling under federal law, and many have never applied under state law, it is not clear whether a university would be chartered as an *educational* organization alone or as an organization which claims exemption under *both* the specific *educational* category and the more general *charitable* category.[80] In the latter event, an objection that the investment activity was not educational might not apply. But even an organization that claims only *educational* status is still—apart from tax categories—a charitable corporation (or a charitable trust); by describing itself as educational, an institution does not lose the right to act like any other charitable corporation or trust. And such an organization, in carrying out its investment functions, is permitted to take steps to avoid participation in violations of law or public policy. Moreover, if resort is had to the educational-climate rationale we have set forth, the noneducational objection is rebutted: the point of the educational-climate rationale is that investment policies of the kind we have proposed *further* the educational mission of the school.

Finally, even if the investment activities we recommend are not deemed consistent with the mission of an institution describing itself as solely educational, that fact does not call for loss of tax exemption. In view of a university's overwhelming preoccupation with educational matters, any "noneducational" investment activity could not reasonably be considered a substantial departure from educational pursuits. Despite language in federal and some state exemption statutes requiring organizations to be "organized . . . exclusively for . . . charitable . . . or educational [etc.] purposes,"[81] an insubstantial amount of nonexempt activity is allowable under federal law and probably state law as well.[82]

As noted at the start of this chapter, if a social investment policy is deemed to violate a university's charter, it may also violate the terms of a tax exemption based on that charter. This point will not, in practice, apply to the many universities that have never bothered to obtain a tax-exemption determination based on their charter or on anything else. Moreover, it seems unlikely that this is the kind of issue in which the Internal Revenue Service or state authorities would express very much interest. In any event, we have already concluded that implementation of the Guidelines we have proposed would not violate the provisions of a university charter.

In sum, we believe that there is no substantial basis for any tax law objection to the investment approach we have proposed.

Conclusion*

The trustees of an institution of higher learning have the authority to adopt the Guidelines we have proposed as an exercise of the

---

*We repeat here two caveats mentioned earlier: first, that the discussion in this chapter focuses, as do our Guidelines, on university action relating to corporate social injury, although we believe our legal conclusions will also apply to the disposition of *non*-social-injury cases (see footnote investment discretion vested in charitable fiduciaries, as an exercise of the power of charitable fiduciaries to avoid participation in violations of law or public policy, or as an exercise of the power of educational fiduciaries to improve the climate for education. The proposed Guidelines are therefore consistent with the legal standards governing the fiduciary behavior of university trustees. Moreover, federal and state tax laws pose no barrier to the adoption of the Guidelines.[83]

Accordingly, there is no legal impediment to the investment policies we have recommended that universities adopt in order to fulfill the "moral minimum" obligation of all investors.

24, p. 196); second, that we cannot guarantee our conclusions against an idiosyncratic state statute or state court precedent or against an aberrational charter provision or donative condition (see p. 137).

Appendix. Suggested Guidelines for the Consideration of Factors Other than Maximum Return in the Management of the University's Investments*

SECTION A: SCOPE OF GUIDELINES AND DEFINITIONS

1. These Guidelines establish criteria and procedures pursuant to which the university will respond to requests from members of the university community that the university take into account factors in addition to maximum economic return when making investment decisions and when exercising its rights as shareholder.
2. The following definitions are used:
   a) *Maximum economic return:* those long-term and short-term financial results, with respect to yield, gain, and safety of capital, which the trustees and the university officers are, at any point in time, seeking to achieve in the management of the university's investments.
   b) *Nonprofit factor:* that which is not exclusively concerned with the production of a maximum economic return.
   c) *Endowment security:* an equity security held for investment as part of the university's endowment funds or other funds (such as loan funds, building and other temporary funds, reserve funds, and current funds) in which securities are held for investment.
   d) *Endowment decision:* a decision relating to the purchase, retention, or sale of an endowment security or to the exercise of shareholder rights with respect to such a security.
   e) *Social injury:* the injurious impact which the activities of a company are found to have on consumers, employees, or other persons, particularly including activities which violate, or frustrate the enforcement of, rules of domestic or international law intended to protect individuals against deprivation of health, safety, or basic freedoms; for purposes of these Guidelines, social injury shall not

---

*These Guidelines are intended to be generally suitable for adoption by most colleges and universities subscribing to the approach outlined in this book. Amendments, of course, will be necessary to meet the needs of each institution, particularly with respect to section C, the procedural section.

consist of doing business with other companies which are themselves engaged in socially injurious activities.

f) *University community:* the faculty, administration, other employees, students, alumni, and trustees of the university.

g) *Finding:* a determination made in accordance with the procedures set forth in section C.

SECTION B: CRITERIA GOVERNING THE USE OF NONPROFIT FACTORS IN ENDOWMENT DECISIONS

1. Selection and retention of endowment securities
    a) Maximum economic return will be the exclusive criterion for selection and retention of the university's endowment securities, except in cases covered by paragraphs 4*(a)*(i) and 4*(a)*(iii) relating to the disposition of securities in certain circumstances.
    b) In no event will an endowment security be selected or retained for the purpose of thereby encouraging or expressing approval of a company's activities, or, alternatively, for the purpose of placing the university in a position to contest a company's activities.
2. Exercise of voting rights
    a) When the university receives proxy materials from the management or other shareholders of a company which set forth propositions dealing with nonprofit factors (for example, propositions requesting the management to change company policies, amending the corporate charter, or altering the structure or management of the company), the university will vote, or cause its shares to be voted, according to the principles set forth in the following paragraphs.
    b) The university will not vote its shares on any resolution which advances a position on a social or political question unrelated to the conduct of the company's business or the disposition of its assets.
    c) The university will vote for a proposition which seeks to eliminate or reduce the social injury caused by a company's activities, and will vote against a proposition which seeks to prevent such elimination or reduction, where a finding has been made that the activities which are the subject of the proposition cause social injury. This paragraph will not apply to any proposition which seeks to eliminate or reduce social injury by means which are found to be ineffective or unreasonable.

  d) With respect to shareholder propositions not covered by paragraphs b and c (for example, propositions not related to the correction of social injury which seek changes in intracorporate relationships or call for an increase or decrease in the company's charitable gifts program or other social welfare activities), the university may, but need not, vote on such propositions.*

3. Exercise of other shareholder rights

  a) Where nonprofit factors are involved in exercising rights, other than the voting rights, of a shareholder (for example, introducing or soliciting support for corporate resolutions, initiating action to elect or defeat directors, initiating or joining in shareholder litigation, making formal or informal representations to corporate management), the university will take action according to the principles set forth in the following paragraphs.

  b) The university will not take any action under this paragraph in order to cause a company to advance a position on a social or political question unrelated to the conduct of the company's business or the disposition of its assets.

  c) The rights referred to in this paragraph will be exercised only in exceptional circumstances where a finding has been made that the proposed university action is directed at a company's activities which cause social injury of a grave character. The foregoing sentence will not apply to the making of formal or informal representations to corporate management; such representations may be made where it is found that the company's activities cause social injury, whether or not of a grave character.

  d) In exercising its rights under this paragraph, the university will not play an initiating role to any extent beyond that which is necessary to ensure that appropriate corrective action is commenced, and it will not take any subsequent action which is not necessary to sustain the appropriate corrective action.

4. Exceptions
Notwithstanding a finding of social injury or grave social injury—

  a) The university will not exercise its shareholder rights

---

*A university that does not wish to vote on these questions until it has developed criteria dealing with them (see discussion in chapter 3) may wish to add this sentence: "Its vote, if any, shall be cast in accordance with criteria to be developed in accordance with paragraph D3."

under the foregoing paragraphs, but will instead sell the securities in question, if a finding is made that—

(i) it is unlikely that, within a reasonable period of time, the exercise of shareholder rights by the university (together with any action taken by others) will succeed in modifying the company's activities sufficiently to eliminate at least that aspect of social injury which is grave in character; or

(ii) it is likely that modification of the company's activities will, within the near future, have a sufficiently unfavorable economic impact on the company to cause the university to sell the securities under the maximum economic return criterion; or

(iii) it is likely that, in the normal course of portfolio management, the securities in question will be sold before the action initiated by the university can be completed.

b) If a finding is made that correction of such social injury will impose a serious competitive disadvantage on the company involved (in relation to other companies in the same industry which cause similar social injury), the university will defer taking shareholder action to compel the company to correct the social injury on a unilateral basis until the university has determined that it will not be possible for it or others to induce the management of the company to bring about industrywide corrective action within the constraints, if any, imposed by the antitrust laws.

c) If a finding is made that correction of such social injury cannot reasonably and appropriately be undertaken by company or industrywide action, as compared to government action, the university will not exercise its shareholder rights under the foregoing paragraphs except to communicate with the management of the company to urge it to seek necessary action from the appropriate government agencies.

d) If a finding is made that, because of extraordinary circumstances, university action otherwise indicated under these Guidelines is likely to impair the capacity of the university to carry out its educational mission (for example, by causing adverse action on the part of governmental or other external agencies or groups, or by causing deep divisions within the university community), then the university will not take such action.

SECTION C: PROCEDURES GOVERNING THE USE OF NONPROFIT FACTORS IN ENDOWMENT DECISIONS

1. The University Investments Council: Membership

   a) There is hereby established the University Investments Council (hereinafter the "council"), which shall be responsible for receiving, studying, and making recommendations to the trustees with respect to requests from members of the university community that the university take action under Section B of these Guidelines.

   b) The council shall be composed of twelve members appointed by the trustees on nomination by the president from each of the components of the university community, in the following numbers: three faculty members, three students, three alumni, one trustee, one administrator, and one employee (other than a faculty member or administrator). The terms of the members shall be fixed by the trustees.

   c) In nominating and electing members of the council, the president and the trustees will take into account the desirability (but not the necessity) of including members—

   (i) who have knowledge of the subject matter areas in which investment questions are likely to arise (such as race relations, public health, environmental control, labor relations, and foreign and military affairs);

   (ii) who have training in one of the various disciplines pertinent to the resolution of the questions which are likely to arise;

   (iii) who, in the case of the faculty, student, and alumni members, are drawn equally from the undergraduate school or college, the graduate school, and the professional schools.

   d) The members of the council shall serve until their successors take office. In the event of a vacancy caused by death, disability, or resignation of a member, the president shall appoint a replacement, who shall serve until the expiration of such member's term and until a successor takes office.

   e) The university treasurer, the university chaplain, and the individual in operational charge of the management of the university's investments (whether a university officer or the chief executive officer of an outside management company) shall be council members *ex officiis.*

2. The University Investments Council: Organization

    a) The council shall choose its own chairman from among its members. The chairman shall serve at the pleasure of the council.

    b) The council may ask individuals, whether or not connected with the university, to attend its meetings as consultants or otherwise provide advice and information.

    c) The council may engage the services of a full-time or part-time research director and other part-time research and clerical assistants.* The university will pay the compensation of these persons and other expenses of the council (such as telephones, postage, reproduction, and purchase of publications) in amounts approved by the trustees on the basis of annual budgets submitted by the council. The university will also provide office space for the research director and his assistants.

    d) The council will have access to the lists of the university's current holdings of endowment securities and to all data compiled by or on behalf of the university with respect to companies in which an investment has been made or contemplated.

    e) The council may establish committees of its members, to serve at the pleasure of the council.

    f) The council may establish rules of procedure, subject to the provisions of these Guidelines.

3. The University Investments Council: Operations

    a) When the council receives from any member of the university community, including a member of the council, a written request for action under these Guidelines, it shall first determine whether the request, on its face and assuming its factual accuracy, appears to meet the criteria established by section B. If the request does not so appear, the individual making the request shall be advised that no further steps will be taken. If the request appears to meet the criteria, the council shall investigate and analyze the request in the light of the criteria established by section B.

    b) In order to carry out its investigation and analysis, the council may—

        (i) refer the request to the research director and/or to a standing or ad hoc committee of the council;

---

*We recognize that not all colleges and universities will wish, or find it possible, to appropriate funds for this purpose.

(ii) seek information and advice from individuals and groups in and out of the university community;

(iii) schedule a meeting to receive information and expressions of opinion from interested individuals and groups in and out of the university community.

c) Before the council submits to the trustees a recommendation for action adverse either to the management of a company or to individuals or groups contesting the management's policies and practices, the council will give full consideration to the facts and arguments advanced by all such parties. Where available written materials do not adequately inform the council, it will seek further information from the parties and may also invite all or any of them to meet with the council or a committee of the council to present further information.

d) Before the council submits to the trustees a recommendation for action based, in whole or in part, on nonprofit factors, the council will ask the individual in operational charge of investment management for an opinion on the effect of such action on the return from the securities in question, and will take this opinion into consideration pursuant to paragraph B4*(a)*(ii).

e) In making the findings on social injury required by section B, the council will take into account not only its own opinions but also the various opinions which appear to be held by substantial numbers of persons within the university community.

f) The council will make its recommendation to the president and the trustees in writing, accompanied by factual findings and an analysis of the question involved. Members of the council or members *ex officiis* who hold dissenting or divergent views may file them in writing with the council's recommendation.

g) The trustees will make the final decisions on all requests for action under these Guidelines. Except in emergency situations, however, the trustees will not take action without receiving a recommendation from the council. The trustees will indulge a presumption in favor of adopting the council's recommendation. It is expected that this presumption will be overcome, and the council recommendation rejected, where the trustees find that the council has not properly applied the Guidelines or that the council's findings of fact are not supported by the available data.

h) The trustees will inform the council in writing of the trustees' action and the reasons for the action.

SECTION D: AMENDMENTS TO THE GUIDELINES

1. The trustees, after consultation with the council, may amend these Guidelines from time to time.
2. The council may, from time to time, submit recommendations to the trustees for amendments to these Guidelines.
3. The council will develop and recommend to the trustees a set of criteria to govern the disposition of cases, arising under paragraph B2*(d)*, involving shareholder proposals based on nonprofit factors but not related to the correction of social injury.

Notes

CHAPTER 1

1. Harvard's Committee on University Relations with Corporate Enterprise issued its report in March 1971; and then President Nathan Pusey stated his position and that of the fellows of the Harvard Corporation later that spring in a letter to the chairman of the university's Governance Commission: "1. Harvard will not make investments which, according to information which has come to our attention and which we believe is reliable, support activities whose primary impact is contrary to fundamental and widely shared ethical principles. 2. Harvard will give due weight, in selecting among investment opportunities, making decisions to retain or sell securities, and voting corporate shares, to the extent to which, according to information which has come to our attention and which we believe is reliable, a business concern acts as a good citizen in the conduct of its business. An important attribute of an investment which is desirable to Harvard is the quality of management and one of the management characteristics we seek is responsiveness to the general welfare and to principles of good business citizenship widely shared in the Harvard community." Additionally, the Corporation has authorized the appointment of a senior administrator to "hear suggestions, conduct investigations and make recommendations . . . on the social behavior of companies in which the university holds stock." The University of Pennsylvania trustees have appointed a committee on corporate responsibility; Princeton, having started with an Ad Hoc Committee on Princeton's Investment in Companies Operating in South Africa, now has a faculty-student Resources Committee to study the problem on a continuing basis; Wesleyan and Stanford have created subcommittees of the trustees' investment committees.

2. See statements by business executives quoted in "The American Corporation under Fire," *Newsweek*, 24 May 1971, pp. 74-83. Studies were initiated in the following areas. *Corporations:* General Motors appointed a public policy committee composed of five GM directors charged with examining the public policy implications of all GM operations. Eastern Gas and Fuel Associates is studying the impact of its operations on various constituencies. *Churches:* The United Church of Christ's Committee on Financial Investments has published a report entitled *Investing Church Funds for Maximum Social Impact* (1970); the Episcopal Church has a Social Criteria Committee on Investments; the General Assembly of the United Presbyterian Church has recently approved the recommendations of a Task Force on Investment Policy. National Boards of a number of other churches including the American Baptist Convention and the United Methodist Church have been actively seeking to develop policies for social investment decision-making. *Foundations:* The Ford Foundation has funded a study of the social aspects of its investments, and the Rockfeller Foundation has a trustee committee studying the same subject. *Insurance*

179

companies: Under the aegis of the Life Insurance Institute, senior officers of several of the leading life insurance companies have held two conferences to discuss the social dimensions of the companies' equity as well as debt investments. Presbyterian Ministers Life has recently announced the adoption of some of the findings of the United Church of Christ report mentioned above. *Mutual funds:* The Dreyfus Leverage Fund polled its members recently to obtain their views on *Campaign GM* and then voted for one of the *Campaign GM* proposals, and the SEC required the Fidelity Trend Fund to include in its proxy materials a shareholder proposal calling on the Fund to analyze all investments and all proxy materials received by the Fund in the light of social criteria. Both the Wellington Management Co. and the Putnam Management Co. have established committees to review socially motivated proposals appearing in the proxy materials of corporations held by the mutual funds they manage. At least two mutual funds have been established for the express purpose of including public policy considerations among stock selection criteria: Pax World Fund and Dreyfus Third Century Fund.

3. Securities and Exchange Commission, *Statistical Series,* no. 2514, 21 April 1971, states that the preliminary computation of the total value of the common and preferred stock held by all educational endowments as of 1970 is $8 billion—a figure which probably includes a small fraction attributable to endowments of primary or secondary schools. One "outside" source asking universities to take shareholder action to affect policies of energy-producing companies is Senator Lee Metcalf of Montana. *Congressional Record,* 28 December 1970, pp. E10733-58.

4. Amherst (1970), Andover-Newton Theological Seminary (1970, 1971), Antioch (1970, 1971), Boston University (1970, 1971), Brown (1970, 1971), Bryn Mawr (1971), Carleton (1971), Haverford (1971), Iowa State (1970), Lincoln (1970), Park College (Kansas City) (1970), Pepperdine (1970), Pomona (1971), Tufts (1970), University of Puget Sound (1971), University of Oregon (1970), Vassar (1971), Wesleyan (1971), Williams (1971). This information and that set forth in the next two footnotes comes from an interview with representatives of *Campaign GM,* from *Non-Profit Report,* June 1971, p. 34, and from Schwartz, "The Public Interest Proxy Contest: Reflections on Campaign GM," 69 *Mich. L. Rev.* 419, 503 (1971). Many other universities may have voted the same way as the institutions listed above and in the succeeding footnotes, but their actions were not made known to the foregoing sources. Another university-related institution which voted its 715,000 shares for one of the *Campaign GM* proposals in 1971 was the College Retirement Equities Fund. *Wall Street Journal,* 3 May 1971, p. 7.

5. Harvard (1971), Rockefeller University (1970), Stanford (1970), Swarthmore (1971), Williams (1970), and Yale (1970).

6. Columbia (1970, 1971), Dartmouth (1971), Harvard (1970), Massachusetts Institute of Technology (1970, 1971), Princeton (1970), Stanford (1971), Swarthmore (1971), University of California (1971), University of Michigan (1970, 1971), University of Pennsylvania (1970).

CHAPTER 2

1. We are indebted for the juxtaposition of these two quotes to Harris Wofford, president of Bryn Mawr College. From some points of view, of course, being the "master instrument of civilized life" is to be convicted of soullessness.

Debate about the corporation in American society and about its desirability in a democratic nation goes back at least to the writers of the American Constitution: Hamilton wanted to give the federal government the power to issue corporate charters for the purpose of promoting trade and industry; Madison felt that corporations would prevent men from participating in public action and were thus a threat to freedom. The debate was resolved in Madison's favor—although in later years some federal charters were issued.

For a brief discussion of the early debates between the Jeffersonians and the Hamiltonians, see Harvey C. Bunke, *A Primer on American Economic History* (New York, 1969), ch. 3, and Edwin M. Epstein, *The Corporation in American Politics* (Englewood Cliffs, N.J., 1969). For fuller discussion, see Oscar and Mary Handlin, "Origins of the American Business Corporation," *Journal of Economic History* 5 (May 1945), and Joseph S. David, *Essays in the Earlier History of American Corporations* vol. 2 (Cambridge, Mass., 1917).

2. Such studies are available, although the issues are certainly not resolved. The modern debate about corporate social responsibility dates from the publication in 1932 of Adolf A. Berle and Gardiner C. Means, *Modern Corporation and Private Property* rev. ed. (New York, 1968). Also in 1932, a debate was carried on in the *Harvard Law Review* between Berle and E. M. Dodd on the responsibility of corporate management. Dodd argued for a broad view in which management is responsible to the public at large. "For Whom Are Corporate Managers Trustees?" 45 *Harv. L. Rev.* 1145 (1932). Berle at that time held to the more traditional view that managers are trustees only for their shareholders. Cf. "For Whom Corporate Managers Are Trustees," 45 *Harv. L. Rev.* 136 (1932); and Berle, *The 20th Century Capitalist Revolution* (New York, 1954), p. 169.

More recent works bearing directly on the problem of corporate social responsibility include: Edward S. Mason, ed., *The Corporation in Modern Society* (New York, 1966); Richard Eells, *The Government of Corporations* (New York, 1962); id., *The Meaning of Business* (New York, 1960), especially chs. 4 and 10-15; Grant McConnell, *Private Power and American Democracy* (New York, 1967); Gordon Bjork, *Private Enterprise and Public Interest* (Englewood Cliffs, N.J., 1969); Howard D. Marshall, ed., *Business and Government: The Problem of Power* (Lexington, Mass., 1970) especially part 1; John Kenneth Galbraith, *The New Industrial State* (Boston, 1967); and Clarence C. Walton, *Corporate Social Responsibilities* (Belmont, California, 1967).

3. Theodore Levitt, "The Dangers of Social Responsibility," in Marshall, ed., *Business and Government*, pp. 22-23.

4. See, for example, the speech delivered by the chairman of General Motors, James M. Roche, at the Executive Club of Chicago, 25 March 1971: "Corporate responsibility is a catchword of the adversary culture that is so evident today. If something is wrong with American society, blame business. Business did not create discrimination in America, but business is expected to eliminate it. Business did not bring about the deterioration of our cities, but business is expected to rebuild them. Business did not create poverty and hunger in our land, but business is expected to eliminate them." Apart from our doubts that business played no role in discrimination in American history, it is clear that Roche does not discern the distinction between corporate responsibility as self-regulation in preventing and correcting social injury, and corporate responsibility as affirmative action in solving all social problems.

5. We are grateful to President Edward Bloustein of Rutgers University for suggesting this terminology and for inviting our attention to its historical antecedents. Further analysis of the distinction between *negative injunctions* and *affirmative duties* is given in the following sections of this chapter.

6. H. L. A. Hart and A. M. Honoré, *Causation in the Law* (Oxford, 1959), p. 59.

7. Jeremy Bentham wrote that " . . . [A]ll rights are made at the expense of liberty. . . . [There is] no right without a correspondent obligation. . . . All coercive law, therefore . . . and in particular all laws creative of liberty, are, as far as they go, abrogative of liberty." "Anarchical Fallacies," in *Society, Law and Morality,* ed. F. A. Olafsson (Englewood Cliffs, N.J., 1961), p. 350. Clearly, Bentham understood that any creation of rights or liberties under the law entailed recognition of an injunction against violating the rights of others.

8. The notion of social injury may also change over time. External norms in the form of government regulations now provide that failure to actively recruit minority group members constitutes discrimination, i.e., is a matter of social injury. See the "affirmative action" requirements, including recruiting measures, imposed on all federal contractors by the federal "contract compliance" regulations. 41 *Code of Federal Regulations,* Section 60-2. At one time, such recruitment was not subject to a negative injunction.

9. We do not suggest that social injury is identical to violation of the legal norms to which we are referring. (In other words, we recognize that some laws themselves cause social injury in the eyes of many persons, and also that not all social injury is prohibited by law.) We are only saying that reference to legal norms will help individuals and institutions to make their own judgments about social injury.

10. See A. M. Rosenthal, *Thirty-Eight Witnesses* (New York, 1964).

11. "Duty to Aid the Endangered Act," *Vt. Stat. Ann.,* ch. 12, § 519 (Supp. 1968). See G. Hughes, "Criminal Omissions," 67 *Yale L. J.* 590 (1958).

12. See, for example, Albert Speer's reflection on his role during the Hitler regime: "For being in a position to know and nevertheless shunning knowledge creates direct responsibility for the consequences—from the very beginning." *Inside the Third Reich* (New York, 1970), p. 19.

13. Failure to respond to need in social situations may also have another effect, equally detrimental to public morality: it suggests to others who might have stepped forward that the situation is really not serious. Thus, two psychologists, John M. Darley and Bibb Latané, after conducting experiments on social reaction to simulated emergencies, concluded that "it is possible for a state of 'pluralistic ignorance' to develop, in which each bystander is led by the apparent lack of concern of the others to interpret the situation as being less serious than he would if alone. To the extent that he does not feel the situation is an emergency, he will be unlikely to take any helpful action." Darley and Latané, *The Unresponsive Bystander: Why Doesn't He Help?* (New York, 1970), cited by Israel Shenker, *New York Times,* 10 April 1971, p. 25. The latter article was based on a separate experiment conducted by Prof. Darley and Dr. C. Daniel Batson at Princeton Theological Seminary designed to determine why people do not help. A group of students were given biblical texts to record, then given individual directions to the recording studio that required them to pass a writhing, gasping student lying in a doorway. It was found that the only significant differentiating factor in determining whether a student stopped to aid was the amount of time he thought he had; those who were told that they were late for the recording session stopped to help much less often (10 per cent) than those who were told that they had sufficient time (63 per cent). It made no statistical difference that half of the seminary students had been given the Parable of the Good Samaritan to record.

14. We do not invoke the Kew Gardens Principle to establish corporate responsibility for clearly self-caused social harm (see n. 63), but rather to demonstrate how shareholders—who may not appear to be directly involved in corporate-caused injury—are obligated to attempt to avert or avoid such injury.

15. The necessity of developing character for moral activity was clearly recognized by the ancient Greeks, who believed that virtue was an art or skill developed through discipline and training over a period of time. The notions of character and virtue have, unfortunately, dropped out of most contemporary discussion of ethics with its emphasis on decision in each moment (rather than on training through time) and on purely instrumental moral decisions (perhaps because of the influence of the social sciences).

16. George Bernard Shaw, *Major Barbara* (Baltimore, 1959), p. 26.

17. Analogously, more affirmative modes of corporate action could be termed the *externalization of benefits.*

18. Quoted by Walton, *Corporate Social Responsibilities,* pp. 101-102.

19. Research and Policy Committee of Committee for Economic Development, *Social Responsibility of Business Corporations* (New York, 1971), p. 44.

20. Levitt, "Dangers of Social Responsibility," pp. 35-36.

21. Milton Friedman, "The Social Responsibility of Business Is to Increase Its Profits," *New York Times Magazine,* 13 September 1970, p. 124. The Friedman position is spelled out in full in *Capitalism and Freedom* (Chicago, 1963).

22. Eugene V. Rostow, "To Whom and for What Ends Is Corporate Management Responsible?" in Mason, *Corporation in Modern Society,* p.

71. Rostow, it may be noted, emphasizes that he is referring to "long-term" profit maximizing. Ibid., p. 70.

23. "Stockholder Interest and the Corporation's Role in Social Policy," in William J. Baumol et al., *A New Rationale for Corporate Social Policy* (New York, 1971), pp. 39, 41, 43.

24. Ibid., pp. 44, 50.

25. Ibid., pp. 55, 41.

26. Ibid., p. 55.

27. Ibid.

28. Committee for Economic Development, *Social Responsibility of Business Corporations,* p. 30.

29. D. E. Schwartz, "Corporate Responsibility in the Age of Aquarius," *The Business Lawyer* 26 (November 1970): 515.

30. Blumberg, "Corporate Responsibility and the Social Crisis," 50 *B.U.L. Rev.* 208 (1970). For a fuller discussion of the legal question, see chapter 5 at pp. 131-32.

31. See Committee for Economic Development, *Social Responsibility of Business Corporations,* pp. 28-29. This statement by the CED's Research and Policy Committee also makes the more general contention that "the pursuit of profit and the pursuit of social objectives can usually be made complementary." Ibid., p. 31.

32. Clem Morgello, "The Price of Virtue," *Newsweek,* 24 March 1971, p. 84.

33. Donaldson, Lufkin & Jenrette, Inc., "General Electric," *Research Bulletin,* 18 April 1971.

34. Berle, "Modern Functions of the Corporate System," 62 *Colum. L. Rev.,* 444. See also in this regard Blumberg, "Corporate Responsibility and the Social Crisis," p. 161. Blumberg cites an editorial in *Fortune* (January 1968), "What Business Can Do for the Cities": "The conventional answer to such questions, volunteered many times by public-spirited businessmen, is that in the long run their inclination to perform good works will also serve to maximize their profits—that, in fact, the profits won't be there unless society is sustained by the kind of good works in question. It is an appealing answer and there is a temptation to swallow it whole; the world would indeed be a wonderful place if profits and good works were so neatly laced together. Unfortunately, however, good works are related more easily to costs than to profits, and where there really is a long-term payoff it will presumably benefit not only the corporation that originally paid for those good works, but other corporations too, including competitors that poured all *their resources into profit maximization.*"

35. Berle, "Modern Functions of the Corporate System," p. 444.

36. Eells, *The Government of Corporations,* p. 97.

37. Mason, *Corporation in Modern Society,* p. 11.

38. Eells, *The Meaning of Modern Business,* chs. 6 and 7. See Neil W. Chamberlain, "The Corporation in Larger Terms," in Chamberlain, *Business and the Cities* (New York, 1970), pp. 505, 508-10.

39. Quoted by Schwartz, "Corporate Responsibility in the Age of Aquarius," p. 518,

40. J. Irwin Miller, "Changing Priorities: Hard Choices, New Price Tags," *Saturday Review*, 23 January 1971.

41. Friedman has made several statements which, depending on how they are interpreted, may lend support to our point of view. For example, in the *New York Times* article already cited, he has this to say about the responsibility of managers: "That responsibility is to conduct the business in accordance with their desires, which generally will be to make as much money as possible while conforming to the basic rules of the society, both those embodied in law and those embodied in ethical custom." Friedman, "The Social Responsibility of Business Is to Increase Its Profits," p. 33.

42. We consider some of these aspects of reasonableness on later pages.

43. See Blumberg quote from *Fortune*, n. 34, *supra*.

44. Henry C. Wallich and John J. McGowan, while doubting the wisdom of "a relaxation in antitrust vigilance . . . as an instrument for the promotion of corporate participation in social policy," state: "[I]t seems a reasonable guess that there would be plenty of room for cooperation by corporations in determining the extent of their social involvement, without incurring risks of antitrust litigation." See Wallich and McGowan, "Shareholder Interest and the Corporation's Role in Social Policy," pp. 58-59. The economic rationale for such corporate collaboration is discussed in William J. Baumol, "Enlightened Self-Interest and Corporate Philanthropy," in Baumol et al., *A New Rationale for Corporate Social Policy*, pp. 3, 11-18.

45. Committee for Economic Development, *Social Responsibility of Business Corporations*, p. 46.

46. "A businessman thoroughly experienced in the give and take of market situations seems peculiarly ill adapted to such a radically different kind of decision making." Manne, "The 'Higher Criticism' of the Modern Corporation," 62 *Colum. L. Rev.* 399, 414 (1962).

47. By *cannot* we refer to the difficulty of solving the problem; or to the regressive impact that the solution might have on, for example, consumers; or to the competitive disadvantage which might result for the corporation.

48. We are grateful to Professor Donald E. Schwartz for drawing this problem to our attention.

49. Levitt, "Dangers of Social Responsibility." pp. 27-28.

50. Epstein, *Corporation in American Politics*, pp. 90-91.

51. Ibid., p. 92.

52. See, for example, S. A. Lakoff, "Private Government in the Managed Society," in J. Roland Pennock and John W. Chapman, *Voluntary Associations*, pp. 170-201.

53. Childs and Cater, *Ethics in a Business Society* (New York, 1954), p. 162.

54. See James C. Tanner's report ·of the tension between Bartlesville, Oklahoma, and the Phillips Petroleum Company: "Phillips Petroleum casts its long shadow on just about every aspect of Bartlesville's community life" and, quoting one businessman: "When Phillips twitches, Bartlesville jumps." (*Wall Street Journal*, 4 August 1966, pp. 1, 9).

55. L. S. Silk, "Business Power Today and Tommorow," *Daedalus* 98

(Winter 1969), p. 188. See also in this regard Robert Heilbroner, *The Limits of American Capitalism* (New York, 1966).

56. Quoted by Howard Taubman, "Rise Seen in Business Aid to the Arts," *New York Times,* 10 February 1971, p. 34.

57. Quoted by Walton, *Corporate Social Responsibilities,* p. 102.

58. A variation on this theme appears in Manne, "The 'Higher Criticism' of the Modern Corporation," p. 416, suggesting that socially motivated corporate "statesmanship" will lead to *coordinated* corporate "statesmanship," and "in time, the government could no longer condone the degree of governmental power that private groups would be exercising, and greater direct governmental control of industry would result."

59. See, for example Huntington, "The Marasmus of the ICC: The Commission, the Railroad and the Public Interest," 61 *Yale L. J.* 467 (1952).

60. McConnell, *Private Power and American Democracy,* p. 7.

61. Karl Kaysen, "The Corporation: How Much Power? How Much Scope?" in Mason, *Corporation in Modern Society,* pp. 99-100.

62. On matters that go beyond self-regulation, we have distinguished in a tentative way between responses to need and attempts to champion one's own point of view, recognizing that the line between the two is most unclear.

63. The four conditions which make up the Kew Gardens Principle (need, proximity, capability, and last resort) would, we think, aid in giving shape to the gray area between negative injunctions and affirmative duties. Where there is some doubt whether or not the corporation has caused the social injury (and whether or not it is thus subject to the negative injunction), the presence of these four conditions should resolve the dilemma. In other words, the special responsibilities which fall on one who has proximity to a critical need, who has the capability of helping, and who is the last resort will often require a corporation to act in a situation in which its self-regulatory duties would otherwise be questionable.

64. Quoted from Berle and Means, *Modern Corporation and Private Property,* by William Cary, *Cases and Materials on Corporations,* 4th ed. (Mineola, New York, 1969), p. 229.

65. Hetherington, "Fact and Legal Theory: Shareholders, Managers, and Corporate Social Responsibility," 21 *Stanford L. Rev.* 249 (1969).

66. Mason, *Corporation in Modern Society,* p. 2.

67. The recent advertisement of New York's Offtrack Betting Corporation is most instructive in this regard: "If you're in the stock market you might find this a better bet." The ad brought strong objections from the president of the New York Stock Exchange.

68. Hetherington, "Fact and Legal Theory," p. 262.

69. Ibid., pp. 260-61.

70. We note that some of the regulations of the New York Stock Exchange have cut in the opposite direction—they appear to be aimed at strengthening the power of the shareholder.

71. Abram Chayes, "The Modern Corporation and the Rule of Law," in Mason, *Corporation in Modern Society,* pp. 40-41.

72. But see the recently decided *Pillsbury* case, cited on p. 194.

73. Manning, Book Review, 67 *Yale L. J.* 1478 (1958); and Cary, *Cases and Materials on Corporations,* p. 245.

74. Hetherington, "Fact and Legal Theory," p. 253.

75. Ibid., p. 253, n. 19.

76. Eells, *Government of Corporations,* especially ch. 2.

77. Hetherington, "Fact and Legal Theory," p. 258. Hetherington makes considerable use in this discussion of Galbraith's analysis of corporate decision-making in *The New Industrial State.* See also Committee for Economic Development, *Social Responsibility of Business Corporations,* p. 22.

78. A somewhat similar list is found in William C. Greenough, "The Power of Institutions," *New York Times,* 2 May 1971, p. 14F.

79. An analysis of the disadvantages of such an approach is set forth in Burton G. Malkiel and Richard E. Quandt, "Moral Issues in Investment Policy," *Harvard Business Review* 49 (March-April 1971): 37, 41-44.

80. The economics team of the Yale seminar—Barr B. Potter, Richard Doernberg, Marc Kahn, and Bert David Collier—reported on the largest sales in stock market history. (See ch. 5, p. 140.) On separate days in 1962, 1964, and 1965, DuPont sold roughly 1.5 million, 4 million, and 3 million shares of GM stock—each sale involving more than the total number of GM shares held in 1968 by 50 of the largest colleges and universities. In 1965 the Ford Foundation sold 6 million shares of Ford Motor stock. In none of these cases were prices depressed for more than one day.

81. Medical Committee for Human Rights v. SEC, 432 F.2d 659 (D.C. Cir. 1970, *cert.* granted), 401 U.S. 973 (1971).

82. Ibid., p. 41.

83. See Patrick H. Allen, "The Proxy System and the Promotion of Social Goals," *The Business Lawyer* 26 (1970): 481-95.

84. For a fuller discussion of the role of institutional shareholders in the *Kodak-FIGHT* confrontation, see C. Powers, *Social Responsibility and Investments* (New York, 1971). pp. 100-01.

85. "Gulf Managers Score Angola Proxy Victory," *The Harvard Crimson,* 29 April 1971, p. 1.

86. "Fidelity Trend Fund Dissident Proposals Get over 10% Backing," *Wall Street Journal,* 26 July 1971, p. 1. The information in the text on A.T.&T. and Potomac Electric Power comes from Donald E. Schwartz, "Towards New Corporate Goals: Co-existence with Society," 60 *Georgetown L. J.* 57, 64 (1971).

87. Malkiel and Quandt, "Moral Issues in Investment Policy," p. 47. See also William L. Cary, "Greening of the Board Room," *New York Times,* 4 August 1971, p. 31: "Companies do not want to appear indifferent during this era of public outcry. As Prof. Louis Loss has pointed out, such proposals are bound to have a healthy indirect impact on corporate management. . . ."

88. A resolution passed by an assembly of the Roman Catholic bishops and priests of Spain in September 1971 declares that priests must speak out on political matters affecting human rights because "[s]ilence in such matters makes the church a guilty accomplice." Richard Eder, "Spanish Church Assembly Asks End of Ties to State," *New York Times,* 17 September 1971, p. 3.

89. We are not suggesting that any legal liability for corporate misconduct attaches to the individual shareholder as a result of the application of
the Kew Gardens Principle. See chapter 5 at pp. 149-50.

90. Bayne, "The Basic Rationale of Proper Subject, 34 *U. Det. L. Rev.*
579 (1957).

91. An apparent example of such harrassment: A recent newspaper account describes a shareholder who apparently owned one share of stock in
each of 27 companies and who made eight shareholder proposals in each
corporation. It cost one of these corporations $50,000 to print and distrib-
ute the proposals and responses to them. At the annual meeting of that
corporation, the shareholder did not appear, and there was no one to move
his proposals (*New York Times,* 21 April 1971). But other information
about that shareholder, Rodney Shields, a Washington lawyer, indicates
that this one incident was a fluke. He showed up at other annual meetings.
And the SEC upheld the propriety of most of his proposals for inclusion in
management proxy statements; half of the companies included them as a
matter of course. One proposal, aimed against discrimination against wom-
en on corporate boards, received considerable shareholder support, was
actively supported by one management group and, in one other company,
was incorporated into the by-laws before the proxy statement was mailed
out. See Council on Economic Priorities, *Economic Priorities Report* 2
(1971):28-30.

92. Securities and Exchange Commission, *Statistical Series,* no. 2514, 21
April 1971.

93. In a substantial number of companies, a small group of institutional
investors (ten or fewer) hold ten per cent or even more of the outstanding
shares. Securities and Exchange Commission, *Institutional Investor Study
Report* 8 (Washington, D.C., 1971):123. The power of these particular
institutions is therefore greater than that of institutional investors in general, but not necessarily greater than that of the corporate management.

94. Friedman, *New York Times Magazine,* 7 July 1970, pp. 32, 124. To
the extent that a socially responsible decision raises the price to a customer
or produces fewer wages for employees, it may well be "against their will,"
but that is true of social and business decisions alike, and in each case the
customers or employees are free to respond in ways which Friedman would
presumably approve: by turning to competitors' products (in the case of
the consumer) and by bargaining for higher wages (in the case of the
employees).

95. *The Harvard Crimson,* 19 May 1970, p. 1.

96. Such as the Council on Economic Priorities and the recently established Corporate Information Center of the National Council of Churches.
Both of these groups also publish source lists of information on corporate
practices.

97. See Schwartz, "The Public Interest Proxy Contest: Reflections on
Campaign GM," 69 *Mich. L. Rev.* 476 (1971): "In earlier times ... [t]he
belief was that the shareholder interest would dictate a narrower focus for
corporate policy and that a more sophisticated and enlightened management would better serve society."

CHAPTER 3

1. "There is no mechanism by which it [the university] can reach a collective position without inhibiting the full freedom of dissent on which it thrives. [There is therefore] a heavy presumption against the university taking collective action or expressing opinions on the social and policital issues of the day, or modifying its corporate activities to foster social or political values, however compelling and appealing they may be." University of Chicago, *The Report of the Committee on the University's Role in Political and Social Action* (Kalven Committee) (1967), p. 2.

2. Yale University, *Report of the President,* 1967-68, p. 37.

3. For example, Quaker schools such as Haverford College maintain a special concern for the Friends' commitment to pacifism through emphasis on research and teaching in the theory and practice of nonviolence; but they welcome to their faculties nonpacifist professors in such disciplines as political science and religion and in no way restrict teaching methodology and content in those fields. The moral and social policy of such institutions regarding investments might be more expansive than the "moral minimum" suggested in chapter 2 as reflected in the Basic Policy.

4. Of course, despite this self-understanding, actions taken by these institutions often signify some value preferences other than the pursuit of academic goals. Indeed, there are those who find a social or moral value choice in almost every decision any university makes. But we here look at what the universities *profess* themselves to be, as the starting point for analysis of the consequences of social or moral investment decisions.

Two different sorts of responses can be given to those who are critical of our decision to accept a profession of institutional purpose that is subject to question. First, it is possible that we will provide an incentive for undertaking a searching reexamination of university self-definition by demonstrating the ways in which the university's ability to act in relation to moral and social concerns is restricted by the *existing* self-definition. Put differently, if we are successful in showing that such a university need not do more—as a responsible institutional investor—than what we outline, unless it alters its self-definition, the educational philosophy which yields that result may be given more careful scrutiny. Second (and this point cuts in another direction), if the university is exempted from a more expansive social investment role because it disavows any social-moral value commitments, this fact may generate pressures on the university to live by this disavowal in various other respects; this prospect of increased consistency may serve as a response to those who object, on *in*consistency grounds, to a university's contention that it does not serve moral or social values.

5. But see, for example, "Institutional Neutrality," *AAUP Bulletin* 55 (1970): 11-13.

6. Both definitions come from *Webster's New World Dictionary of the American Language* (New York, 1953), s.v. "neutral."

7. Indeed, *neutrality* is a term which in other settings as well has tended to obscure rather than clarify issues concerning the relationships between insititutions. Mr. Justice Goldberg called attention to this in his

opinion concerning state-church problems relating to education: ". . . un-tutored devotion to the concept of neutrality can lead to invocation or approval of results which partake not simply of that noninterference and noninvolvement with the religious which the Constitution commands, but of a brooding and pervasive, or even active, hostility to the religious. Such results are not compelled by the Constitution, but, it seems to me, are prohibited by it." Abingdon School District v. Schempp, 374 U.S. 203.

8. The American Association of University Professors and the courts increasingly have been concerned with giving academic freedom a more specific explication in this country. See Richard Hofstadter and Walter P. Metzger, *The Development of Academic Freedom in the United States* (New York, 1955); and "Academic Freedom," *Law and Contemporary Problems* 28 (see especially Ralph F. Fuchs "Academic Freedom—Its Basic Philosophy, Function and History," pp. 431-47); and Louis Joughin, *Academic Freedom and Tenure* (Madison, Wisc., 1969).

9. The nature of the Academic Context is discussed in greater detail on pp. 73-75.

10. *AAUP Bulletin* 27 (1942): 84-87.

11. *New York Times Magazine,* 22 March 1970. Although Kristol is a critic of most attempts to get the universities institutionally involved in social affairs, he proceeds in the same paragraph to argue a case which is in some ways analogous to the view we espouse: "Such organization and administration do indeed imply responsibilities. More precisely, they imply a responsibility—the responsibility to be reasonable with regard to the interests and sensibilities of other organizations and other people. And I don't think they imply anything more than that."

12. Moreover, educational institutions with religious or moral commit-ments are not the only ones which have declined to invest in stocks of liquor or tobacco producers. Many of the institutions we are not discussing also have done so. We surmise that trustees of these institutions have acknowledged either that ownership entails some sort of responsibility for the actions of companies in which they invest, or that a university should not receive profits made from the sale of certain products deemed socially injurious or immoral. In either case, the neutrality position has been eroded, even in the investment arena.

13. It is possible that the term might be invoked to deal with other questions. For example, it might be employed to try to prevent the uni-versity from getting involved in areas where it is incompetent. If so, this issue is addressed on pp. 83-85.

14. *The Harvard Crimson,* 7 October 1969, p. 5.

15. See ch. 3, n. 8, *supra.*

16. This concern is expressed in the Report of the Stanford University Trustees Ad Hoc Committee on Investment Responsibility (13 April 1971, p. 1) as follows: "Most important, we as trustees have no moral or legal right to speak for diverse elements of the Stanford Community on contro-versial social, economic and political issues or to use the name or the resources of the University to support particular positions on such issues except where the issues directly impinge upon the activities of the Universi-

ty." The Committee did not, however, foreclose all social investment activities.

17. See, for example, the *Final Report of the Yale University Study Commission on Governance,* 1971, pp. 46-48.

18. This condition entails few implications as to the size of an educational institution or the number of persons it serves. It requires only that those who make up the learning and teaching community receive adequate support for their endeavors and that the university or college be large enough and sufficiently heterogeneous to allow for the representation and investigation of what Brewster has called the "alternatives of importance." Yale University, *Report of the President,* 1967-68, p. 37.

19. Robert Paul Wolff, *The Ideal of the University* (Boston, 1969).

20. Letter to the Editor, *Cornell Daily Sun,* 17 April 1968. Commitment to the maintenance of freedom from external domination has been expressed as follows by Yale President Kingman Brewster: "We will of course seek assistance for programs of teaching and research which we ourselves initiate. We do not intend to permit the contributor to dictate how that work shall be pursued." Yale University, *Report of the President,* 1969-70, p. 18.

21. As chapter 5 will show, such a focus helps to support one of three alternative legal justifications for our approach. Both this provision and the previous one (locating final decision-making power outside the academic sector) were employed to help develop the distance strategy for preventing the *internal* threat to the academic Context.

22. We recognize that such a safety clause allows a university, in an extreme case, to fail to honor its "moral minimum" responsibilities in order to save itself, whereas we have not admitted that a business corporation can avoid *its* self-regulatory obligation in order to stay in business. The differential treatment is based, in part, on the fact that the university—as compared to the corporation—does not itself *cause* the social injury to take place and therefore has a somewhat lower order of responsibility for the correction of the social injury. Thus, if a university itself caused social injury as a direct result of its operations, it might not be entitled to the benefit of a safety clause excusing it temporarily from the obligation to correct such injury.

23. This position is taken in the recent report of the Harvard University Committee on Governance, entitled *The Nature and Purposes of the University:* "In the long run, mankind needs some institution dedicated to the search for truth and the value of intellectual inquiry. The university has undertaken the job, and although it may have been diverted, it has a greater potential for fulfilling the role than any other human institution. We must reaffirm our commitment to the search for truth as the central value of the university. We must rekindle our faith in the capacity of people to choose wisely for themselves within a climate of honest search. We must renew our dedication to a university community wherein the dialectic of detached inquiry and passionate involvement is safeguarded and preserved."

24. "What Business Is the University In?" *New York Times Magazine,* 22 March 1970, p. 30 ff.

25. Ibid., p. 106. A similar point of view is expressed by Edward H. Levi, President of the University of Chicago: "The University is the home of ideas. Many of these ideas are incorrect and foolish. Many are persuasive, dangerous and devastatingly impractical. Faculties are not selected for a general ability to be prudent and practical." *Point of View: Talks on Education* (New York, 1969), p. 53.

26. Here we take issue not only with Kristol but with Callicles, who said: "For philosophy, you know, Socrates, is a pretty thing if you engage in it moderately in your youth; but if you continue in it longer than you should, it is the ruin of man. For if a man is exceptionally gifted and yet pursues philosophy far on in life, he must prove entirely unacquainted with all the accomplishments requisite for a gentleman and a man of distinction. Such men know nothing of the laws in their cities or of the language they should use in their business associations both public or private with other men, or of human pleasures and appetites, and in a word they are completely without experience of men's character. And so when they enter upon any activity public or private they appear ridiculous, just as public men, I suppose, appear ridiculous when they take part in your discussions and arguments." (Plato *Gorgias* 484C-D). A substantial part of Plato's work can be viewed as an effort to dissolve this dichotomy.

27. Yale University, *Report of the President, 1967-68*, p. 29.

28. University of Chicago, Kalven Committee, *Report*, p. 3.

29. We make reference here to the particular injury under discussion, not to the overall character of the impact of the corporation on society.

30. It is not clear that there would be such losses or costs. Extra transaction costs would not be imposed unless this sale was additive to the amount of portfolio turnover normally taking place. As for losses in return, we do not mean to ascribe to the stock-selection process a level of efficiency which implies that a security sold for social reasons could never be replaced by an equally remunerative substitute; our seminar's economics team reported that, at least through 1968, the fifteen university endowments examined in a recent Ford Foundation report did not enjoy anywhere near that degree of efficiency. In any event, however, requiring the portfolio managers to unload securities—and search for equally promising substitutes—whenever controversy arises or social injury is detected would considerably encumber, and therefore probably impair, the endowment management process.

31. See pp. 25-26, 53, 91.

32. An example might be a corporation whose sole or primary product caused social injury (i.e., one that made only cigarettes, assuming hypothetically that it had been determined that cigarettes were deemed to cause grave social injury).

33. This rationale for a heavily restricted divestment policy prompts the question whether a university, on similar purity grounds, should refuse gifts from a notoriously antisocial donor. (In our seminar we talked about a charitable contribution to a university from Murder, Inc.) Although the present study does not address this issue, we pause to suggest that it might initially be resolved on a basis similar to the investment questions we have been considering; i.e., the acceptance of the gift from a company or in-

dividual might turn on the question of whether or not the university thereby encouraged or acquiesced in the continuation of the practices considered harmful. A decision on this issue would involve such questions as whether the donor (if an individual) is living or dead; whether publicity accompanies the gift, thus lending a measure of respectability to the donor ("Murder, Inc., Donates New Gymnasium to Yale"); and whether acceptance of a particular type of contributed property (e.g., a cigarette factory) implied the recipient's approval of the donor's activity. Where, as in most cases, it is decided that acceptance will *not* constitute encouragement or acquiescence, then the sole remaining question is whether it is improper to receive money from a tainted source. Our tentative view is that this is not a situation which calls for action on purity grounds; the gift consitutes a one-time transaction, not involving an enduring affiliation as in the case of stock ownership.

34. Indeed, two economists who are concerned about the costs of university social investment actions believe there will be no such costs in respect to one major element of the policy we propose: "There are, of course, ways in which the portfolio might be employed without incurring any costs. Voting proxies is one obvious example. In cases such as the recent attempt by *Campaign GM* to create a Shareholders' Committee of Corporate Responsibility, it would be difficult to argue that a university or pension fund would injure itself by voting in favor of the proposals. . . . Of course, one might argue that the resulting change in the corporate structure of GM would, over the long run, reduce its net earnings. But one can just as realistically argue that the ability of GM to remain a profitable enterprise depends on its success in ameliorating the pollution caused by automobiles." Malkiel and Quandt, "Moral Issues in Investment Policy," p. 46.

Phillip I. Blumberg agrees that many recent socially oriented shareholder proposals "would have involved no material cost to the corporation." Phillip I. Blumberg, "The Politicalization of the Corporation," *The Business Lawyer* 26, no. 5 (1970): 1565. He states, however, that some other shareholder proposals—such as those introduced by church groups at the Gulf Oil, Kennecott Copper, American Metal Climax, and General Motors meetings in 1971—would "produce significant loss to the corporation." Ibid., p. 1566. But the impact on an institutional shareholder of such a corporate loss might not be significant. The loss may turn out to be short-term rather than long-term; moreover, despite the loss incurred by the single corporation, the change in corporate practice may increase the returns recovered by an entire industry or by the corporate sector as a whole—and thus redound to the overall advantage of a diversified institutional shareholder. These points are discussed in greater detail in chapter 2 at pp. 31-34.

35. Reported in the *Harvard Bulletin,* 15 June 1970, pp. 17-19.

36. See discussion of *Campaign GM,* p. 55.

37. As a revised draft of this book was being prepared in March 1971, Harvard's Austin Committee (Committee on University Relations with Corporate Enterprise) released its report recommending an approach roughly similar to the one we outline.

CHAPTER 5

1. Dodd, "For Whom Are Corporate Managers Trustees?" 45 *Harv. L. Rev.* 1145, 1148, 1160 (1932).

2. See Blumberg, "Corporate Responsibility and the Social Crisis," 50 *B. U. L. Rev.* 157, 174 (1970).

3. 13 N.J. 145, 154, 98 A.2d 581, 586, *appeal dism'd*, 346 U.S. 861 (1953).

4. One of the issues that the courts have thus managed to avoid involves the relative rights of majority and minority shareholder interests in corporations. If a management were found to have taken a position for exclusively social purposes, the next question might be whether the shareholders had ratified the action. If the court found that the majority of the shareholders had explicitly or implicitly assented, would this action offend any legally protectable expectations of the dissenting shareholders? I.e., does this minority have a right not to be surprised by avowedly social initiatives? If so, the existence of such a right may provide a reason for interpreting ambiguous state statutes to prevent such social initiatives—and even to prevent a shareholder majority from amending the corporate charter to permit these initiatives. But why does the minority have such a right? This issue of shareholder expectations remains to be explored in the literature of this field.

5. Hetherington, "Fact and Legal Theory: Shareholders, Managers, and Corporate Social Responsibility," 21 *Stan. L. Rev.* 248, 257-58 (1969). One case that might be cited for the proposition that profit maximization is required is Dodge v. Ford Motor Company, 204 Mich. 459, 170 N.W. 668 (1919), where the court compelled payment of a dividend which had been "arbitrarily" withheld to permit the company to sell cars more cheaply; the court concluded that the directors had neither the long-term nor the short-term interests of the shareholders at heart, but instead had a "general purpose and plan to benefit mankind at the expense of [shareholders]"— that the directors meant "to shape and conduct the affairs of [the] corporation for the merely incidental benefit of the shareholders and for the primary purpose of benefiting others. . . ." 204 Mich. 507-07, 170 N.W. at 684. These extreme conclusions go well beyond any findings a court is likely to make in a case where the issue is the legality of corporate action to correct social injury.

In any event, we know of only one other case—decided while this book was being printed—suggesting a profit-maximizing imperative. In State *ex rel.* Pillsbury v. Honeywell, 191 N.W.2d 406 (1971), a shareholder was denied the right to inspect corporate books in order to communicate with other shareholders about Honeywell's production of antipersonnel bombs used in Vietnam; the Minnesota Supreme Court held that petitioner had not shown a "purpose germane to his or Honeywell's economic interest . . ." Id. at 413. The case's precedential force is limited by the fact that it arose in the shareholder-inspection context (where this court and others have been wary of harassment) and by the finding (emphasized by court) that the petitioner bought his stock solely for the purpose of influencing

Honeywell's policies—a course of action, it will be noted, which a university may not pursue under our Guidelines.

6. Blumberg, "Corporate Responsibility and the Social Crisis," p. 206.

7. Sylvia Martin Foundation, Inc. v. Swearingen, 260 F. Supp. 231 (S.D.N.Y. 1966); background facts appear in Memorandum of Defendant Standard Oil Company in Support of Its Motion under Rules 12(b) and 56.

8. Shlensky v. Wrigley, 95 Ill. App. 2d 173, 237 N. E. 2d 776 (1968). See also Kelly v. Bell, 254 A. 2d 62, 74 (Del. Ch. 1969), *aff'd* 266 A. 2d 878 (1970).

9. If a successful shareholder proponent of socially corrective conduct bases his action on explicitly *non*business considerations, does that fact undermine the corporation's later efforts to defend the action under the business-purpose rationale? The only commentator who has discussed the question thinks not. See Schwartz, "The Public-Interest Proxy Contest," p. 474.

10. Ballantine on *Corporations,* § 42, p. 119 (1946).

11. With respect to charter amendments prohibiting certain products, see Medical Committee for Human Rights v. SEC, 432 F.2d 659 (D.C. Cir. 1970), *cert.* granted, 401 U.S. 973 (1971) (resolution asking the board of the Dow Chemical Co. to consider a charter amendment prohibiting manufacture of napalm). A by-law requiring additional disclosure was proposed by the Project on Corporate Responsibility in Round II (1971) of *Campaign GM.*

12. See 2 Loss, Securities Regulation 905-6 (2d ed. 1961); Schwartz, "The Public-Interest Proxy Contest," p. 440. One case suggests, in passing, that federal securities laws may create for shareholders a substantive *federal* right to vote on important questions, perhaps including by-law changes, SEC v. Transamerica Corp., F.2d 511, 518 (2d Cir. 1947), but the suggestion has not been implemented in subsequent case law. Whatever limitations there may be on the power of shareholders to mandate corporate action, there is authority for the proposition that the shareholders may call a meeting to express their opinions on the conduct of corporate affairs. Auer v. Dressel, 306 N.Y. 427, 432, 118 N.E.2d 590, 593 (1954).

13. Rule 14a-8(c), 17 C.F.R. § 240, 14a-8(c) (1970). Alternative formulations of the shareholder proposal rules have been suggested in Note, "Liberalizing SEC Rule 14a-8 through the Use of Advisory Proposals," 80 *Yale L. J.* 845 (1971); Note, "Proxy Rule 14a-8: Omission of Shareholder Proposals," 84 *Harv. L. Rev.* 700 (1971); and Schwartz, "The Public-Interest Proxy Contest," pp. 520-29.

14. Senator Muskie has introduced a bill which would limit this rule to cases where the "matter or action is not within the control" of the corporation. S. 4003, U.S. Congress, Senate, 92d Cong., 2d sess., 23 June 1970.

15. This point was made in a paper prepared for the Yale seminar by Richard W. Cass, dated 30 January 1970. And see Medical Committee for Human Rights v. SEC, *supra;* but also see Peck v. Greyhound Corp., 97 F. Supp. 679 (S.D.N.Y. 1951).

16. Peck v. Greyhound, *supra,* approved—without explanation—the SEC's reliance on an earlier, less formal version of this rule to permit the

management to bar "a recommendation that management consider the advisability of abolishing the segregated seating system in the south." For a one-year (1955-56) sampling of the kinds of proposals excluded by the management under this rule, see Bayne, "The Basic Rationale of *Proper Subject*," 34 *U. Det. L. J.* 575, 598-99 (1957).

17. In Brooks v. Standard Oil Co., 308 F. Supp. 810 (S.D.N.Y. 1969), the court held—on proper-subject-for-shareholders grounds—that the company did not have to include in its proxy materials a resolution calling on the company to intensify its efforts to encourage the development of petroleum reserves beneath the continental shelves; the resolution also asked the company to encourage creation of a world regime with jurisdiction over underseas mineral resources. The authorities relating to the proper-subject-for-shareholders rule are listed in Eisenberg, "Access to the Corporate Proxy Machinery," 83 *Harv. L. Rev.* 1489, 1523 (1970).

18. 432 F. 2d 659 (D.C. Cir. 1970), *cert.* granted 401 U.S. 973 (1971).

19. 432 F. 2d at 680-81.

20. This assumes that the generally silent state courts do not come up with a different view on the question of what may properly come before a shareholders' meeting. The issue might arise if the chairman of a stockholders' meeting rules a socially oriented resolution out of order (despite its inclusion in the management proxy materials), and if the proponent of the resolution then asked a state court to rule on the legality of the chairman's action. See also the *Pillsbury* case, n. 5, *supra*.

21. *Restatement of Trusts 2d,* § 174 (1959). As it originated in the case of Harvard College v. Amory, 26 Mass. (9 Pick.) 446, 461 (1830), the rule read as follows: "All that can be required of a trustee to invest, is, that he shall conduct himself faithfully and exercise a sound discretion. He is to observe how men of prudence, discretion and intelligence manage their own affairs, not in regard to speculation, but in regard to the permanent disposition of their funds, considering the probable income as well as the probable safety of the capital to be invested." The rule is now embodied in statutes in several states. For example, Conn. Gen. Stat., § 45-88 provides that trust property may be "invested . . . in any bonds or stocks or other securities, selected by the trustee . . . with the care of a prudent investor." See note 23, below.

22. Conn. Gen Stat., § 47-2, applicable to those gifts to a university which are true endowment gifts (principal to be permanently preserved), provides: "All estates granted for the maintenance of . . . school of learning . . . shall forever remain to the uses to which they were granted, according to the true intent and meaning of the grantor, and to no other use whatever." See also St. Joseph's Hospital v. Bennett, 281 N.Y. 115, 22 N.E. 2d 305 (1939).

23. Note, however, that the prudent-man rule is not so universally cited as a directive to directors of charitable corporations as it is in the case of trustees of charitable trusts; some statutes pertaining to charitable corporations do not expressly invoke the rule. See A. Scott, *The Law of Trusts,* § 389, at 2998-99 (1967).

24. We refer to the Guidelines rules that require a university to participate in correcting corporate social injury, not to the cases where the uni-

versity is asked to vote on socially oriented proxy questions *not* involving social injury. Although the Guidelines impose limits on the university's range of action in dealing with the latter cases, we have left to later university action the formulation of detailed criteria for such cases (see Guidelines, paragraphs B2(d) and D3). Accordingly, the present legal discussion does not purport to provide firm conclusions relating to these non-social injury cases. However, we believe that all of the discussion and conclusions set forth in this chapter, with the exception of the illegality rationale, will probably apply to—and therefore sustain the propriety of—university action on such non-social injury questions.

25. Quoted in Peter Landau, "Do Institutional Investors Have a Social Responsibility," *Institutional Investor* 4 (July 1970):25, 87.

26. Ibid.

27. Wallich and McGowan, "Stockholder Interest and the Corporation's Role in Social Policy," cited and discussed in chapter 2, pp. 31-32.

28. The college-university data come from the annual Boston Fund report on the holdings of these fifty schools.

29. See discussion at pp. 142-43.

30. A. Scott, *Abridgement of the Law of Trusts,* § 380 at 691-92 (1960).

31. Carrel v. State *ex rel* Brown, 11 Ohio App. 281, 287 (1919), discussed in Blake, "The Impact of Divestiture Rules on the Discretion of Charitable Fiduciaries" 19 (unpub. MS 1964).

32. Scott, *The Law of Trusts,* § 193.1 at 1594.

33. Cary and Bright, "The Income of Endowment Funds," 69 *Colum. L. Rev.* 396, 407-08 (1969). See also idem, *The Law and Lore of Endowment Funds* (New York, 1969), p. 19, concluding that with respect to the administration of charitable corporations, "corporate principles are applied . . . with remarkable uniformity by the courts of all states. . . ."

34. Note, "The Charitable Corporation," 65 *Harv. L. Rev.* 1168, 1173 (1951). See also Karst "The Efficiency of the Charitable Dollar: An Unfulfilled State Responsibility," 73 *Harv. L. Rev.* 433, 435 (1960).

35. Att'y Gen. of N.Y., *1951 Annual Report,* pp. 159, 191.

36. In Connecticut, the "[c]ourts on occasion may find a gift to a charitable corporation a gift in trust, especially where an alternative holding would result in the bequest being devoted to noncharitable uses," Burt, "The Law and Yale's Endowment" 4 (unpub. MS 1970), but the Connecticut courts have enunciated the general proposition that "[a] gift to a . . . charitable corporation to aid in carrying out the purposes for which it was organized . . . does not create a trust in any legal sense." Pierce v. Phelps, 75 Conn. 83, 86, 52 A. 612, 613 (1902).

37. Ballantine on *Corporations,* § 83, at 224 (1946). In Connecticut, for example, applying this doctrine to the directors of a charitable corporation (Yale), the Supreme Court of Errors in 1899 struck down New Haven's effort to tax rich students' dormitories. The city claimed that these facilities represented a "perversion of the purposes of the college." The court held that the Fellows of the Yale Corporation were not subject to judicial scrutiny with respect to their administrative decisions. Yale University v. New Haven, 71 Conn. 316, 42 A. 87 (1899).

38. Scott, *Abridgement*, §377, at 689. Similar language appears in *Restatement of Trusts 2d*, §377 (1959). See also Bogert, *Handbook of the Law of Trusts*, §48 (4th ed. 1963). Examples of violations of public policy not embodied in law are found in *In re Hill's Estate*, 119 Wash. 62, 204 P. 1055, *aff'd on rehearing*, 207 p. 689 (1922) holding that a trust to support the teaching of homeopathic medicine was invalid because such teaching was detrimental to public health; In re Sterne, 147 Misc. 59, 263 N.Y. Supp. 304 (Surr. Ct., N.Y. Co. 1933) holding that a trust provision requiring physicians to split fees was invalid because fee-splitting violated public policy; Nourse v. Merriam, 62 Mass. (8 Cush.) 11 (1851) holding "contrary to good morals and public policy" an educational bequest which provided that descendants of certain persons must be excluded from school. A similar illegality doctrine, also referring to violations of public policy, is found in the law relating to the enforcement of contracts. See 6A Corbin on *Contracts*, § § 1375-76 (1962).

39. Although this rule originated in the law of charitable trusts, its applicability to charitable corporations, as well as charitable trusts, is demonstrated in such cases as Mormon Church v. United States, 136 U.S. 1 (1890) sustaining the power of Congress to dissolve a church corporation which advocated polygamy, and Zeissweiss v. James, 63 Pa. 465 (1870) holding illegal a legacy for an incorporated Infidel Society. The one *legislative* declaration of charitable invalidity on public policy grounds cited by Scott, Michigan Stat. Ann., § 27.3178(71a), as added by Pub. Acts 1951, no. 157, refers to devises or bequests to any association *or corporation*. And the "cy pres" doctrine, which recites illegality as a ground for not enforcing the precise terms of charitable instruments, applies to corporations as well as trusts. Scott, *The Law of Trusts*, §399, at 3086.

40. See Scott, *Abridgement*, § 374.

41. See Scott, *The Law of Trusts*, § 167.

42. Colonial Trust Co. v. Brown, 105 Conn. 261, 286, 135 A. 555, 564 (1926). The restrictions were also economically harmful to the beneficiaries of the private trust, but the court placed at least equal weight on the adverse consequences for "the public welfare."

43. *Restatement of Trusts 2d*, §227, comment *q*, at 537. *Illegal* as used in this section refers to §166 of the *Restatement* rather than § 377, but the usage appears to be identical. It should be noted that in Scott's explication of the term *illegal* in §166, most of the cases cited involved administrative rather than substantive trust provisions. Scott, *Abridgement*, §166, at 313-14.

44. Scott, "Control of Property by the Dead," 65 *U. Pa. L. Rev.* 632, 655 (1917).

45. *Restatement of Trusts 2d*, §227, comment *q*, at 537.

46. Ibid., § 166, comment *e*, at 350.

47. Scott, *The Law of Trusts*, § 167.1, at 1282.

48. *Restatement of Trusts 2d*, §166(1), (2), at 347.

49. An analogy is found in the area of constitutional litigation over de facto school segregation. The courts have generally been unwilling to order school districts to adopt racial-balancing measures to correct de facto segregation. The cases are summarized in A. Bickel, *The Supreme Court and the*

Idea of Progress (New York, 1970), pp. 131, 196. At least one reason for this response has been a judicial reluctance to command government action which is not color-blind. Yet where school districts have initiated such racial-balancing measures on their own, the courts have sustained them in the face of constitutional challenges to their non-color-blind character. Ibid., pp. 118-19, 194. Here again, the legal *power* of responsible officials to take certain action appears to be broader than their *obligation* to act.

50. This participation question was addressed in chapter 2; so that this legal discussion may be comprehensible without the need to refer back, we discuss the question again here.

51. And except, to a limited extent, for the shareholders of national banks.

52. The law on this last point is summarized in Hetherington, "Fact and Legal Theory," pp. 248, 249.

53. Medical Committee for Human Rights v. SEC, 432 F.2d 659, 680-81 (D.C. Cir., 1970), *cert. granted,* 401 U.S. 973 (1971).

54. Hetherington, "Fact and Legal Theory," pp. 250-63.

55. Ibid., p. 251; see this chapter at pp. 132-35.

56. In many states charter amendment requires both a resolution by the board of directors and shareholder approval. Cary, *Cases and Materials on Corporations* p. 160 (4th ed. 1969); Henn, *Handbook of the Law of Corporations,* § 215, at 426 (2d ed. 1970).

57. Scott, *Abridgement,* § 377, at 689.

58. We refer to the abundant literature on consistency or inconsistency between judicial "legislation" and the democratic process. Corbin discusses this question as it arises in a context analogous to ours: the context of judicial nonenforcement of contracts on public policy grounds. Corbin on *Contracts,* § 1376.

59. Scott, *Abridgement,* § 62, at 155.

60. Ibid.

61. The bricking-up case is Brown v. Burdett, 21 Ch. D.667 (1882), and the clock case is Kelly v. Nichols, 17 R.I. 306 (1891); these and other cases involving "capricious purposes" are discussed in Scott, *Abridgement,* § § 62.14, 124.7. The cases involving relief of a trustee from liability are discussed in ibid., § 62.15.

62. Gulliver, Clark, Lusky, and Murphy, *Cases and Materials on Gratuitous Transfers,* p. 763 (1967). See Perry, *Trusts and Trustees,* § 379 (6th ed. 1911); Vierling, "The Rule Against Perpetuities Applied to Trusts," 9 *St. Louis L. Rev.* 286 (1924): Note, "Limitations on the Settlor's Power of Disposition and Control of the Trust Property," 12 *Corn. L. Q.* 549, 551 (1927) ("the rule against perpetuities developed from judge-made public policy molded into a definite form by generations of precedent").

63. Unless, of course, the expenditure of such income was necessary to advance the stated purposes of the charitable organization—a point discussed in the next part of this chapter.

64. Scott, *Abridgement,* § 192.

65. *Restatement of Trusts 2d,* § 227(c); see also ibid., comment *q.*

66. In re London, 104 Misc. 372, 377, 171 N.Y. Supp. 981, 983 (Sur. Ct. N.Y. Co. 1918), *aff'd mem.* 187 App. Div. 952, 175 N.Y. Supp. 910

(1919). See also In re Bayly, [1944] N.Z.L.R. 868 (Sup. Ct.) (permissible for trustees to invest in government war loans paying a lower rate of interest than necessary to meet expenses, so as to minimize public reaction against large estates).

67. Scott, *The Law of Trusts,* § 227.14, at 1848.

68. Hutton v. *West Cork Ry.,* [1883] 23 Ch. D. 654, 673 (C.A.).

69. McGeorge Bundy, "One Day Before," *Yale Alumni Magazine,* 33 (June 1970): 26-27.

70. President's Commission on Campus Unrest, *Survey of Campus Incidents as Interpreted by College Presidents, Faculty Chairmen, and Student Body Presidents* (Oct. 1970), p. 32.

71. In a recent poll of Harvard alumni, a majority of the respondents recommended that the university consider public-policy implications when making investments. *Harvard Alumni Bulletin,* 15 June 1970, pp. 17-19; see chapter 3 for discussion.

72. Speech printed in "Managing Endowment Capital," *Proceedings of the Endowment Conference,* 1 April 1970, pp. 109-10.

73. *Int. Rev. Code of 1954* § 4944(c), as added by § 101(b) of the Tax Reform Act of 1969, P.L. 91-172.

74. At least on the general question of what kind of social investment policy a university should adopt, alumni attitudes may not be very different from those of students and faculty. See the results of the Harvard poll, discussed in chapter 3 at p. 104.

75. The preamble to Yale University's 1745 charter expressly envisions action to protect its long-term future; it recites that the petitioners for the charter had asked that what is now called the Yale Corporation be granted "such other additional Powers and Privileges . . . as shall be necessary for the Ordering and Managing the said school in the most Advantageous and beneficial Manner for the promoting all good literature in the present *and succeeding Generations"* (emphasis supplied).

76. Paragraph B4(c) of the Guidelines states: "If a finding is made that correction of such social injury cannot reasonably . . . be undertaken by company or industrywide action, as compared to government action, then the university will . . . communicate with the management of the company to urge it to seek necessary action from the appropriate government agencies." Even where the appropriate agency is a legislative one, we do not think that urging a company to seek corrective legislation will constitute, for the university, a substantial amount of legislative activity, particularly if it happens only rarely.

77. The reference is to Judge Hand's decision in Slee v. Commissioner, 42 F. 2d 184, 185 (2d Cir. 1930), involving the legislative activities of the American Birth Control League.

78. Reg. § 1.501(c)(3)-1(d)(2).

79. Reg. § 1.501(c)(3)-1(d)(3).

80. These are federal tax exemption categories, *Int. Rev. Code* § 501(c)(3). The state categories vary. New York and Connecticut exemption statutes list both the *educational* and *charitable* categories. N.Y. Real Prop. Tax Law, § 420, subd. 1; Conn. Gen. Stat., § 12-81(7). Under the (federal) Internal Revenue Code a university need not apply for an exemp-

tion determination before enjoying the benefits of exemption; this is also true in nineteen states. A. Balk, *The Free List* (New York, 1971), p. 165. The Tax Reform Act of 1969 requires universities and certain other exempt organizations to file a document categorizing themselves in certain respects, but this form does not refer to the *charitable* or *educational* categories. Int. Rev. Serv. Form 4653 (June 1970), p. 1.

81. *Int. Rev. Code,* §501(c)(3). The New York and Connecticut Statutes cited in note 80, *supra,* contain similar language.

82. With respect to federal law, the precedents are summarized in House Committee on Ways and Means, *Report on Tax Reform Act of 1969* (1969), p. 33. With respect to state law, see People *ex rel.* Marsters v. Rev. Saletyni Missionaries, Inc., 409 Ill. 370, 99 N.E. 2d 186 (1951) (holding that if the primary use of a charity's property is for exempt purposes, an inconsistent incidental use will not forfeit the exemption); Yale Univ. v. Town and City of New Haven, 17 Conn. Supp. 166, 180 (Ct. of Common Pleas, New Haven Co. 1950) ("it does not appear that in this connection the word 'exclusively' has been strictly construed," citing Yale Univ. v. New Haven, 71 Conn. 316 (1899)); People *ex rel.* Clarkson Mem. College v. Haggett, 191 Misc. 621, 624 (Sup. Ct., St. Lawrence Co. 1948) ("A cursory consideration of the authorities demonstrates that this state has not bound itself to a strict construction of the word 'exclusively' ").

83. In this chapter we have not discussed two categories of legal questions that might be pertinent for some investment programs or some investors but are unlikely to arise under the proposed Guidelines. (a) Because our Guidelines preclude sale of securities for noneconomic reasons, except in very limited situations, and particularly because we have not recommended any sales in concert with other investors, this chapter does not treat the possible legal objections to such concerted action under the antitrust and securities laws. (We do not mean to suggest, however, that these objections would be well founded.) The antitrust aspects were studied in an unpublished paper prepared for the Yale seminar by Olof Hellen, dated December 20, 1970; see also Bird, "Sherman Act Limitations on Noncommercial Refusals to Deal," 1970 *Duke L. J.* 247. (b) Should a university find it advisable publicly to explain its reasons for taking shareholder action, we assume that it would be scrupulously careful to be accurate. For this reason, because truth is a defense to an action for defamation, and because we believe such a lawsuit to be highly unlikely, we have not devoted further space to this question. We note, however, that in the event of inadvertent inaccuracy, the university would probably be protected by the rule of qualified privilege against liability for any statement not found to be "malicious" or knowingly or recklessly false. See W. Prosser, *Handbook of the Law of Torts,* § §115, 116, 118 (1971); see also Rosenbloom v. Metromedia, 403 U.S. 29 (1971).

Index